MAMMALS OF SOUTHERN AFRICA

To Him who created them all

A Field Guide

MAMMALS OF SOUTHERN AFRICA

Burger Cillié

FRANDSEN PUBLISHERS
SANDTON
1987

First impression 1987
Published in South Africa by Frandsen Publishers (Pty) Ltd
P O Box 122, Fourways 2055

© Burger Cillié

Design by Robin Frandsen
Reproduction and typesetting by Pointset (Pty) Ltd, Randburg
Printed and bound by Interpak Natal, Pietermaritzburg

ISBN 0 620 10367 1

FOREWORD

Those of us who live in Southern Africa are fortunate in that we can still escape from the built-up areas in which we live and enjoy the freer life of the outdoors. In doing so an increasing number of people are finding enjoyment and relaxation in viewing wildlife either in National Parks or reserves, by the roadside as they travel by car, or even in some cases on their own properties. Southern Africa has much to offer those people for among its rich heritage of wildlife it supports over 290 species of mammals ranging in size from tiny mice to elephants. Not all of these are readily seen for many are small and live nocturnal lives but, from this wide spectrum of mammals, the author has chosen 83 which anyone has, at some time or another, a good chance of seeing. These are illustrated by the superb series of colour photographs most of which he has gathered over many years of painstaking and patient work in the field. These photographs, together with the descriptions given in the text, should be of the greatest assistance to the observers in identifying accurately the animal they have seen. The observation is then made the more interesting by the information the author provides on a range of facets of the life history of the species being dealt with, including its habits, the food it eats and information on breeding.

The result is a concise and invaluable field guide, beautifully illustrated, which will surely be appreciated by anyone interested in our mammalian fauna.

Reay H.N. Smithers
Transvaal Museum
Pretoria

CONTENTS

GAME RESERVES AND NATIONAL PARKS

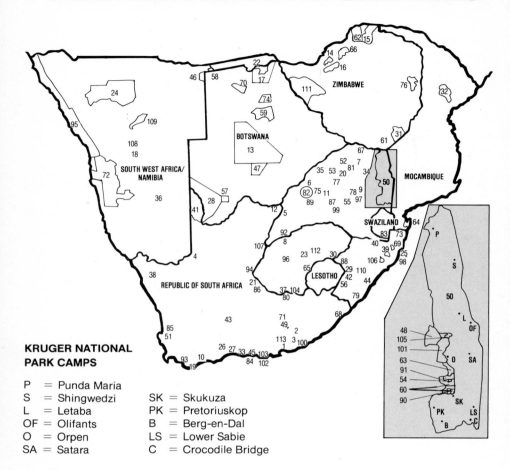

KRUGER NATIONAL PARK CAMPS

P   = Punda Maria
S   = Shingwedzi
L   = Letaba
OF = Olifants
O   = Orpen
SA = Satara

SK = Skukuza
PK = Pretoriuskop
B   = Berg-en-Dal
LS = Lower Sabie
C   = Crocodile Bridge

1. Addo (Patterson)
2. Amalinda (Adelaide)
3. Andries Vosloo (Grahamstown)
4. Augrabies (Kakamas)
5. Barberspan
6. Ben Alberts (Thabazimbi)
7. Ben Lavin (Louis Trichardt)
8. Bloemhof Dam (Bloemhof)
9. Blyde River Canyon (Bourke's Luck)
10. Bontebok (Swellendam)
11. Borokalano (Assen)
12. Botsalano (Mafikeng)
13. Central Kalahari

14. Chete (Siabuwa)
15. Chewore (Mwami)
16. Chizarira (Siabuwa)
17. Chobe (Kasane)
18. Daan Viljoen (Windhoek)
19. De Hoop (Bredasdorp)
20. Doorndraai Dam (Potgietersrus)
21. Doornkloof (Petrusville)
22. Eastern and Western Caprivi
23. Erfenis Dam (Theunissen)
24. Etosha
25. False Bay
26. Gamkaberg (Oudtshoorn)

27. Gamkapoort (Oudtshoorn)
28. Gemsbok (Lokwabe)
29. Giants Castle (Escourt)
30. Golden Gate (Clarens)
31. Gona-re-zhou (Triangle)
32. Gorongosa (Vila Machado)
33. Goukamma (Knysna)
34. Hans Merensky (Letsitele)
35. Hans Strijdom Dam (Ellisras)
36. Hardap (Mariental)
37. Hendrik Verwoerd Dam (Spring-
    fontein)
38. Hester Malan (Springbok)
39. Hluhluwe
40. Itala (Louwsburg)
41. Kalahari Gemsbok
42. Kamberg (Nottingham Road)
43. Karoo (Beaufort West)
44. Kenneth Stainbank (Durban)
45. Keurboom (Plettenberg Bay)
46. Khaudum (Rundu)
47. Khutse (Takatokwane)
48. Klaserie (Hoedspruit)
49. Kommandodrift (Cradock)
50. Kruger Park
51. Langebaan
52. Langjan (Vivo)
53. Lapalala (Marken)
54. Londolozi (Next to Kruger Park)
55. Loskop Dam (Groblersdal)
56. Loteni (Himeville)
57. Mabuasehube (Tshabong)
58. Mahonga (Andara)
59. Makgadikgadi Pan (Gweta)
60. Mala Mala (Next to Kruger Park)
61. Malapati (Triangle)
62. Mana Pools (Makuti)
63. Manyeleti (Next to Kruger Park)
64. Maputo Elephant (Bela Vista)
65. Maria Maroka (Thaba Nchu)
66. Matusadona (Kariba)
67. Messina
68. Mkambati (Lusikisiki)
69. Mkuzi
70. Moremi (Okavango delta)

71. Mountain Zebra (Cradock)
72. Naukluft (Walvis Bay)
73. Ndumu
74. Nxaipan (Kanyu)
75. Nyala Ranch (Koedoeskop)
76. Nyanga (Mutare)
77. Nylsvley (Naboomspruit)
78. Ohrighstad Dam (Lydenburg)
79. Oribi Gorge (Port Shepstone)
80. Oviston (Venterstad)
81. Percy Fyfe (Potgietersrus)
82. Pilansberg (Sun City)
83. Pongola (Golela)
84. Robberg (Plettenberg Bay)
85. Rocherpan (Velddrif)
86. Rolfontein (Petrusville)
87. Roodeplaat Dam (Pretoria)
88. Royal Natal (Bergville)
89. Rustenburg
90. Sabi-Sabi (Next to Kruger Park)
91. Sabi-Sand (Next to Kruger Park)
92. S.A. Lombard (Bloemhof)
93. Salmons Dam (Stanford)
94. Sandveld (Hopetown)
95. Skeleton Coast (Torra Bay)
96. Soetdoring (Dealesville)
97. Sterkspruit (Lydenburg)
98. St. Lucia
99. Suikerbosrand (Heidelberg)
100. Thomas Baines (Grahamstown)
101. Timbavati (Next to Kruger Park)
102. Tsitsikama Coastal
103. Tsitsikama Forest
104. Tussen-die-riviere (Bethulie)
105. Umbabat/Motswari (Next to
     Kruger Park)
106. Umfolozi (Mtubatuba)
107. Vaalbos (Kimberley)
108. Von Bach (Okahandja)
109. Waterberg Plateau (Otjiwarongo)
110. Weenen (Colenso)
111. Whange
112. Willem Pretorius (Winburg)
113. Zuurberg (Kirkwood)

TABLE OF WHICH ANIMALS OCCUR IN WHICH PARKS OR RESERVES	1. South African Hedgehog	2. Chacma Baboon	3. Vervet Monkey	4. Samango Monkey	5. Bat-eared Fox	6. Wild Dog	7. Cape Fox	8. Side-striped Jackal	9. Black-backed Jackal	10. Cape Clawless Otter	11. Honey Badger	12. Striped Polecat	13. African Civet	14. Large-spotted Genet	15. Suricate	16. Yellow Mongoose	17. Water Mongoose	18. Banded Mongoose	19. Dwarf Mongoose	20. Aardwolf	21. Brown Hyaena	22. Spotted Hyaena	23. Cheetah	24. Leopard	25. Lion	26. Caracal	27. Serval	28. Small Spotted Cat	29. African Wild Cat	30. Elephant	31. Cape Mountain Zebra	32. Hartmann's Mountain Zebra	33. Burchell's Zebra	34. Square-lipped Rhinoceros	35. Hook-lipped Rhinoceros	36. Rock Dassie	37. Antbear
1. Addo			•		•		•							•						•						•			•						•	•	•
2. Amalinda			•			•		•	•		•				•	•												•								•	
3. Andries Vosloo	•	•	•					•	•		•				•	•				•						•			•						•	•	•
4. Augrabies		•	•		•			•	•	•	•				•	•	•			•						•			•						•	•	•
5. Barberspan	•					•			•		•		•		•												•	•									•
6. Ben Alberts	•	•	•					•											•					•		•			•					•	•		
7. Ben Lavin								•								•	•	•	•					•										•		•	•
8. Bloemhof Dam	•							•			•				•																			•	•		
9. Blyde River Canyon														•			•	•	•																	•	
10. Bontebok		•			•		•		•		•		•			•								•		•							•			•	•
11. Borokalano	•	•	•			•		•	•							•	•		•					•		•			•						•		•
12. Botsalano	•					•		•			•					•		•	•							•			•					•	•		•
13. Central Kalahari				•			•		•			•	•		•	•		•		•	•		•	•	•	•	•										•
14. Chete		•	•			•		•				•	•	•			•	•	•		•		•	•	•				•	•			•			•	•
15. Chewore		•	•	•		•		•				•	•	•			•	•	•		•	•	•	•	•				•	•			•			•	•
16. Chizarira		•	•		•	•		•			•	•	•					•	•		•	•	•	•	•				•	•			•			•	•
17. Chobe		•	•		•	•			•		•	•	•	•		•		•	•		•		•	•	•				•	•			•				
18. Daan Viljoen	•	•			•		•		•						•	•				•	•		•	•		•		•	•			•				•	•
19. De Hoop		•					•				•					•	•														•					•	
20. Doorndraai Dam	•	•	•					•	•		•	•		•		•	•	•	•					•					•						•	•	•
21. Doornkloof	•		•		•			•	•		•				•	•	•			•	•			•		•			•								•
22. Eastern Caprivi		•	•			•		•		•	•	•	•			•		•	•		•		•	•	•				•	•			•				•
23. Erfenis Dam						•			•		•		•		•	•	•			•						•			•				•				•
24. Etosha	•	•	•		•	•	•	•	•		•	•	•		•	•		•	•	•	•	•	•	•	•	•	•	•	•			•	•		•	•	
25. False Bay																	•	•	•														•				
26. Gamkaberg		•			•		•		•							•					•			•		•		•			•					•	•
27. Gamkapoort		•			•		•		•	•		•				•				•				•		•			•							•	•
28. Gemsbok					•	•	•		•			•	•		•	•				•	•			•	•	•	•		•	•							•

38. Warthog	39. Bushpig	40. Hippopotamus	41. Giraffe	42. Black Wildebeest	43. Blue Wildebeest	44. Lichtenstein's Hartebeest	45. Red Hartebeest	46. Bontebok	47. Blesbok	48. Tsessebe	49. Blue Duiker	50. Red Duiker	51. Common Duiker	52. Springbok	53. Klipspringer	54. Damara Dik-dik	55. Oribi	56. Steenbok	57. Cape Grysbok	58. Sharpe's Grysbok	59. Suni	60. Impala	61. Black-faced Impala	62. Grey Rhebok	63. Roan Antelope	64. Sable Antelope	65. Gemsbok	66. Buffalo	67. Kudu	68. Sitatunga	69. Nyala	70. Bushbuck	71. Eland	72. Reedbuck	73. Mountain Reedbuck	74. Waterbuck	75. Lechwe	76. Puku	77. Pangolin	78. Cape Hare	79. Scrub Hare	80. Ground Squirrel	81. Tree Squirrel	82. Springhare	83. Porcupine

TABLE OF WHICH ANIMALS OCCUR IN WHICH PARKS OR RESERVES	1. South African Hedgehog	2. Chacma Baboon	3. Vervet Monkey	4. Samango Monkey	5. Bat-eared Fox	6. Wild Dog	7. Cape Fox	8. Side-striped Jackal	9. Black-backed Jackal	10. Cape Clawless Otter	11. Honey Badger	12. Striped Polecat	13. African Civet	14. Large-spotted Genet	15. Suricate	16. Yellow Mongoose	17. Water Mongoose	18. Banded Mongoose	19. Dwarf Mongoose	20. Aardwolf	21. Brown Hyaena	22. Spotted Hyaena	23. Cheetah	24. Leopard	25. Lion	26. Caracal	27. Serval	28. Small Spotted Cat	29. African Wild Cat	30. Elephant	31. Cape Mountain Zebra	32. Hartmann's Mountain Zebra	33. Burchell's Zebra	34. Square-lipped Rhinoceros	35. Hook-lipped Rhinoceros	36. Rock Dassie	37. Antbear
29. Giants Castle		•							•	•										•			•	•	•											•	
30. Golden Gate	•	•							•	•			•			•				•				•	•	•					•					•	
31. Gona-re-zhou		•	•		•	•			•		•	•	•			•	•		•	•	•	•	•	•	•	•		•	•			•	•	•	•	•	•
32. Gorongosa		•	•	•	•	•		•			•	•	•			•	•	•		•		•	•	•	•	•		•	•			•		•		•	
33. Goukamma		•				•				•			•	•																						•	
34. Hans Merensky		•	•		•			•	•		•	•	•	•		•	•		•	•	•	•	•	•	•	•										•	•
35. Hans Strijdom Dam	•	•	•						•	•	•	•	•			•	•	•		•			•	•	•	•										•	•
36. Hardap		•			•		•		•		•				•	•				•	•		•	•	•	•				•						•	•
37. Hendrik Verwoerd Dam	•						•				•				•	•	•							•	•				•							•	
38. Hester Malan		•			•		•		•		•				•	•				•			•	•	•				•							•	
39. Hluhluwe		•	•	•		•			•		•	•				•	•		•	•	•	•	•	•	•	•			•			•	•	•	•	•	•
40. Itala		•									•					•							•											•	•	•	•
41. Kalahari-Gemsbok	•	•			•	•	•		•		•	•			•	•				•	•	•	•	•	•	•											•
42. Kamberg																																				•	
43. Karoo		•	•					?	•						•	•	•			•				•		•		•	•	•						•	•
44. Kenneth Stainbank																	•																•			•	
45. Keurboom		•	•			•			•	•		•											•	•												•	
46. Khaudum		•	•		•	•		•	•	•	•	•	•			•		•	•	•	•	•	•	•	•	•			•	•			•				•
47. Khutse					•				•		•				•	•			•	•			•	•	•	•			•	•							•
48. Klaserie		•	•		•			•	•	•	•	•	•	•		•	•			•		•	•	•	•	•			•	•			•	•		•	•
49. Kommandodrift	•	•	•		•			•	•	•		•				•	•	•		•				•				•								•	•
50. Kruger		•	•	•	•	•		•	•		•	•	•			•	•	•		•	•	•	•	•	•	•			•	•		•	•	•	•	•	•
51. Langebaan			•				•		•			•				•	•							•		•											
52. Langjan	•	•	•		•				•		•	•	•			•	•							•	•				•							•	•
53. Lapalala	•	•	•						•				•				•		•	•				•				•					•	•		•	•
54. Londolozi		•	•			•		•	•	•	•	•	•	•		•	•					•	•	•	•	•			•	•			•	•	•	•	•
55. Loskop Dam						•						•				•	•	•	•														•	•		•	
56. Loteni												•																								•	

38. Warthog	39. Bushpig	40. Hippopotamus	41. Giraffe	42. Black Wildebeest	43. Blue Wildebeest	44. Lichtenstein's Hartebeest	45. Red Hartebeest	46. Bontebok	47. Blesbok	48. Tsessebe	49. Blue Duiker	50. Red Duiker	51. Common Duiker	52. Springbok	53. Klipspringer	54. Damara Dik-dik	55. Oribi	56. Steenbok	57. Cape Grysbok	58. Sharpe's Grysbok	59. Suni	60. Impala	61. Black-faced Impala	62. Grey Rhebok	63. Roan Antelope	64. Sable Antelope	65. Gemsbok	66. Buffalo	67. Kudu	68. Sitatunga	69. Nyala	70. Bushbuck	71. Eland	72. Reedbuck	73. Mountain Reedbuck	74. Waterbuck	75. Lechwe	76. Puku	77. Pangolin	78. Cape Hare	79. Scrub Hare	80. Ground Squirrel	81. Tree Squirrel	82. Springhare	83. Porcupine
			•				•		•				•	•		•								•				•				•	•	•	•								•		•
			•						•					•			•							•				•				•		•					•					•	
•	•	•	•		•	•							•	•	•		•	•		•			•		•	•		•	•	•	•	•	•	•		•			•		•		•	•	•
•	•	•			•	•							•	•	•		•			•	•	•			•	•		•	•		•	•	•	•	•				•				•	•	•
•							•						•	•			•										•					•							•	•	•	•		•	•
			•	•		•							•	•			•															•			•				•	•	•			•	
•	•	•	•		•								•	•	•		•			•		•						•	•	•	•	•	•		•				•		•		•	•	•
•			•			•					•		•	•			•															•													
•					•	•							•	•			•											•				•							•	•	•	•		•	•
			•		•	•						•		•			•							•								•	•	•					•		•				
			•		•	•							•	•			•			•								•				•			•				•	•					
													•	•	•						•									•	•													•	•
										•			•					•																											
•			•		•				•			•		•		•						•	•		•							•	•						•		•				
•					•								•	•			•									•				•		•		•					•		•			•	
•	•	•			•								•	•		•			•	•		•	•		•	•		•	•		•	•	•	•	•		•		•		•		•	•	•
			•				•		•				•	•			•										•					•			•				•	•	•		•	•	•
•	•	•	•		•	•			•			•		•		•						•	•		•	•	•	•	•	•	•	•	•	•	•	•			•	•	•	•	•	•	•
													•				•	•														•	•												
•	•	•	•		•				•				•	•			•					•	•		•	•	•	•	•	•	•	•	•	•	•				•		•	•	•	•	•
•	•		•	•		•							•	•			•											•	•	•		•	•	•	•	•				•		•			•
														•			•	•														•	•												
•	•	•	•		•				•				•	•			•			•		•	•		•	•	•	•	•	•	•	•	•	•	•				•	•	•	•	•	•	•
			•		•				•				•	•			•											•	•	•		•	•	•	•	•				•				•	
													•					•	•													•	•												

Column headers (species):

38. Warthog
39. Bushpig
40. Hippopotamus
41. Giraffe
42. Black Wildebeest
43. Blue Wildebeest
44. Lichtenstein's Hartebeest
45. Red Hartebeest
46. Bontebok
47. Blesbok
48. Tsessebe
49. Blue Duiker
50. Red Duiker
51. Common Duiker
52. Springbok
53. Klipspringer
54. Damara Dik-dik
55. Oribi
56. Steenbok
57. Cape Grysbok
58. Sharpe's Grysbok
59. Suni
60. Impala
61. Black-faced Impala
62. Grey Rhebok
63. Roan Antelope
64. Sable Antelope
65. Gemsbok
66. Buffalo
67. Kudu
68. Sitatunga
69. Nyala
70. Bushbuck
71. Eland
72. Reedbuck
73. Mountain Reedbuck
74. Waterbuck
75. Lechwe
76. Puku
77. Pangolin
78. Cape Hare
79. Scrub Hare
80. Ground Squirrel
81. Tree Squirrel
82. Springhare
83. Porcupine

TABLE OF WHICH ANIMALS OCCUR IN WHICH PARKS OR RESERVES	1. South African Hedgehog	2. Chacma Baboon	3. Vervet Monkey	4. Samango Monkey	5. Bat-eared Fox	6. Wild Dog	7. Cape Fox	8. Side-striped Jackal	9. Black-backed Jackal	10. Cape Clawless Otter	11. Honey Badger	12. Striped Polecat	13. African Civet	14. Large-spotted Genet	15. Suricate	16. Yellow Mongoose	17. Water Mongoose	18. Banded Mongoose	19. Dwarf Mongoose	20. Aardwolf	21. Brown Hyaena	22. Spotted Hyaena	23. Cheetah	24. Leopard	25. Lion	26. Caracal	27. Serval	28. Small Spotted Cat	29. African Wild Cat	30. Elephant	31. Cape Mountain Zebra	32. Hartmann's Mountain Zebra	33. Burchell's Zebra	34. Square-lipped Rhinoceros	35. Hook-lipped Rhinoceros	36. Rock Dassie	37. Antbear
85. Rocherpan				•		•									•	•																				•	
86. Rolfontein	•	•	•		•		•		•	•					•	•	•				•	•		•		•		•	•				•	•		•	•
87. Roodeplaat Dam	•						•				•		•		•	•					•							•	•				•			•	•
88. Royal Natal		•					•	•																•		•	•		•							•	
89. Rustenburg	•	•	•		•				•						•						•			•					•							•	
90. Sabi-Sabi		•	•			•		•	•		•		•	•		•	•	•	•	•		•	•	•	•	•		•	•				•			•	•
91. Sabi-sand		•	•			•		•	•		•		•	•		•	•	•	•	•		•	•	•	•	•		•	•				•			•	•
92. S.A. Lombard	•						•		•				•		•	•					•																•
93. Salmons Dam		•					•						•			•	•									•										•	
94. Sandveld			•				•		•	•			•			•	•											•	•							•	
95. Skeleton Coast		•			•		•		•	•						•	•	•	•		•	•	•	•				•	•			•			•		•
96. Soetdoring	•		•				•		•	•			•		•	•					•					•	•		•				•			•	•
97. Sterkspruit													•			•				•	•															•	
98. St. Lucia			•	•				•	•	•	•					•	•	•	•		•	•		•									•			•	
99. Suikerbosrand	•	•					•		•							•	•				•	•					•	•								•
100. Thomas Baines	•		•												•	•												•						•		•	•
101. Timbavati		•	•		•		•	•	•			•	•	•		•	•			•		•	•	•	•	•		•	•			•				•	•
102. Tsitsikamma Coastal		•	•						•	•	•		•	•			•							•		•										•	
103. Tsitsikamma Forest		•	•						•	•	•		•	•			•							•		•										•	
104. Tussen-die-Riviere	•	•	•		•		•		•	•			•		•	•	•				•					•		•	•				•	•		•	•
105. Umbabat/Motswari		•	•			•		•	•		•		•	•		•	•			•		•	•	•	•	•		•	•				•			•	•
106. Umfolozi		•	•			•			•	•	•						•			•		•	•	•	•	•							•	•	•	•	•
107. Vaalbos		•	•		•		•		•	•			•			•					•	•				•		•	•				•	•		•	•
108. Von Bach	•	•			•		•		•	•			•		•						•	•		•		•	•					•				•	•
109. Waterberg Plateau	•	•	•		•		•		•	•	•		•			•	•			•	•	•	•	•		•	•							•		•	
110. Weenen							•					•																					•	•	•		
111. Whange	•	•	•		•	•			•				•			•		•	•		•	•	•	•		•	•	•	•			•		•	•	•	•
112. Willem Pretorius		•	•				•		•	•			•		•	•	•	•		•				•									•	•	•	•	•
113. Zuurberg	•	•	•		•				•	•	•	•	•	•		•				•				•		•		•			•					•	•

Species columns (left to right):

38. Warthog
39. Bushpig
40. Hippopotamus
41. Giraffe
42. Black Wildebeest
43. Blue Wildebeest
44. Lichtenstein's Hartebeest
45. Red Hartebeest
46. Bontebok
47. Blesbok
48. Tsessebe
49. Blue Duiker
50. Red Duiker
51. Common Duiker
52. Springbok
53. Klipspringer
54. Damara Dik-dik
55. Oribi
56. Steenbok
57. Cape Grysbok
58. Sharpe's Grysbok
59. Suni
60. Impala
61. Black-faced Impala
62. Grey Rhebok
63. Roan Antelope
64. Sable Antelope
65. Gemsbok
66. Buffalo
67. Kudu
68. Sitatunga
69. Nyala
70. Bushbuck
71. Eland
72. Reedbuck
73. Mountain Reedbuck
74. Waterbuck
75. Lechwe
76. Puku
77. Pangolin
78. Cape Hare
79. Scrub Hare
80. Ground Squirrel
81. Tree Squirrel
82. Springhare
83. Porcupine

INTRODUCTION

This book has been compiled to serve as a manual for anyone wishing to know more about the fauna of Southern Africa. It is not intended as a scientific text book, although the facts are all zoologically correct. Primarily, the purpose is to assist in identifying each animal. For this reason it was decided to make use of colour photography which must be the truest representation of proportional size, shape and colour.

Two photographs, usually depicting male and female, are shown of each animal, as the sexes differ in many instances. Distinctive characteristics of animals likely to be confused with each other, are also highlighted.

Geographically the book covers the entire southern African territory south of the Kunene and Zambesi rivers, including the Caprivi Strip.

All the larger land mammals, from the smallest antelope to the elephant, appear in this book, in addition to the more commonly known smaller mammals.

A map indicating the positions of all the major and better known reserves in the territory is shown, also tables indicating which animals appear in the various reserves.

The record tusk and horn sizes given in this book are the African records.

Mammals of Southern Africa is an invaluable quick concise reference work for use in the field and will assist all who read it to know the pertinent facts concerning the fauna of this rich zoological territory.

ACKNOWLEDGEMENTS

Firstly, I wish to thank Dr. Reay H.N. Smithers who was enthusiastic about the idea of such a book from the beginning, and assisted me in every way. His encouragement, patience, suggestions and aid in compiling the text, are greatly appreciated.

Many thanks to the nature conservation organisations – the Departments of Nature Conservation in the Cape Province, Orange Free State, Transvaal and South West Africa/Namibia, the Natal Parks Board, the National Parks and Tourism Departments of Botswana, Zimbabwe and Moçambique, the Wildlife Society of Southern Africa and the Endangered Wildlife Trust for information regarding the location of animals.

My heartfelt thanks go to all the wildlife photographers, who generously provided the photographs used in this book.

I would also like to express my thanks to the following persons for their share in preparation:

Marthinus Schoeman and Oscar Neumeyer for the translation and finishing of the English text.

Adelia Carsten for the Afrikaans linguistic corrections and Joy Frandsen for the English amendments.

Robin Frandsen for drawing the animals for the identi-index and for sketching the spoor of each animal.

Daleen Muller for typing the final manuscript.

My thanks go to all the family and friends for their interest and suggestions, especially my wife and children for their patience and encouragement during the preparation of the book.

Many thanks to Frandsen Publishers for their trust in accepting the book.

Above all I give thanks to my Creator for the privilege of presenting to others a portion of His wonderful creation in this manner.

To Him be the glory.

Burger Cillié
December 1986

▲1　　　　　　　　　　　　　　　　　　　　2▼

1 SOUTH AFRICAN HEDGEHOG
Atelerix frontalis
(Suid-Afrikaanse krimpvarkie)

Description: The body is covered with small short spines from the forehead, behind the ears, across the back and down the flanks. The spines are ringed with black and white or dull yellow, some being completely white. The legs and tail are covered with grey-brown hair. The face is framed with white hair across the forehead above the eyes and underneath the ears. The rest of the face is dark brown or black. The snout is pointed.

Sexual dimorphism: None.

Habitat: Found in a variety of habitats where sufficient food and dry shelter is available.

Habits: Hedgehogs are mainly nocturnal but are sometimes seen during the day after rain. During the day they rest curled up like a ball under thick layers of leaves, dense grass or bushes, or in holes. The resting place changes daily. The only semi-permanent resting place is where females keep their young, until they are able to move with her. their eyesight is bad but they have a keen sense of smell, locating their food even if it is situated just below the surface of the soil which they then dig out. During the winter they become torpid, rarely emerging from their resting place.

Voice: Snuffle, snort and growl or a high pitched alarm call.

Food: Beetles, termites, millipedes, locusts, moths, earthworms, small birds, lizards and snails.

Gestation period: ± 5 weeks.

Breeding: October – April.

Number of young: 1 – 9.

Mass: 236 g – 480 g (9 – 16 oz).

Length: ± 20 cm (± 8″).

Life expectancy: ± 3 years.

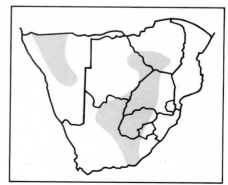

▲3♂   4♀▼

2 CHACMA BABOON *Papio ursinus*
(Kaapse bobbejaan)

Description: The Chacma Baboon is characterised by the first third part of the tail being carried upwards and the remainder hanging down. The rump displays pinkish callosities. The face is elongated and the nostrils are located at the very end of the snout. The legs are long and the feet are longer than the hands. The colour varies from greyish dull yellow, through shades of brown, to almost black in the older males. Newly born young are dark in colour with pink faces.

Sexual dimorphism: The males are larger and more aggressive than the females.

Habitat: Very adaptable to any habitat but prefer mountainous or well wooded areas.

Habits: Form troops of up to 70 individuals, with a distinct hierarchy consisting of a leader supported by one or more dominant males with their family groups. From early childhood positions in this hierarchy are being continuously contested. By night the baboons sleep on high cliffs or in tall trees, leaving early in the morning to forage and returning to their sleeping places in the late afternoon. The males act as guards while the troops forage. The very young cling to their mother's bellies, but ride on their mother's backs when older.

Voice: Growl, bark and a warning "bawchom" from the males, screaming and chattering from the young.

Food: Wild fruit, berries, insects, scorpions and meat.

Gestation period: ± 6 months.

Breeding: Throughout the year.

Number of young: One, seldom two.

Mass: ♂ 27 – 44 kg (59 – 97 lb).
♀ 14 – 17 kg (30 – 37 lb).

Shoulder height: ♂ ± 71 cm (± 28″).
♀ ± 61 cm (± 24″).

Life expectancy: ± 18 years.

Tail: ± 60 cm (± 23″)

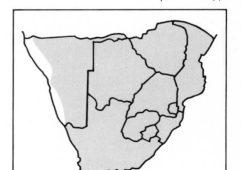

F   H

▲5♂

6♀▼

3 VERVET MONKEY *Cercopithecus aethiops*
(Blouaap)

Description: A small light-grey monkey with a conspicuously long tail. The belly and flanks are lighter than the upper parts. The face is black and framed with white hair. The feet and the tip of the tail are dark in colour. The male's genitalia is blue. It is distinguished from the Samango Monkey by being smaller and lighter in colour and is without the black shoulders and legs.

Sexual dimorphism: Males are larger than females.

Habitat: They prefer woodland, especially on river banks and also favour proximity to human habitation.

Habits: These swift tree climbers, which still occur outside conservation areas, are diurnal and form troops numbering up to 20. A hierarchy exists in their troops which is not as well developed as with Baboons. They display aggressive attitudes towards lower ranked animals in the troops, by chasing them, or sometimes only by an aggressive lifting of the eyebrows. At night they sleep in tall trees preferring to forage in the early morning. They rest during the heat of day returning in the early afternoon to their sleeping places.

Voice: They utter chattering and stuttering sounds and the emergency call of the young is a high scream.

Food: Mainly wild fruit, flowers, leaves, seeds, insects, birds and eggs.

Gestation period: ± 7 months.

Breeding: Throughout the year.

Number of young: One, rarely two.

Mass: ♂ 3,8 – 8,0 kg (8 – 18 lb).
♀ 3,4 – 5,2 kg (7 – 11 lb).

Shoulder height: ♂ ± 31 cm (± 12″).
♀ ± 26 cm (± 10″).

Life expectancy: ± 12 years.

Tail: ± 65 cm (± 26″).

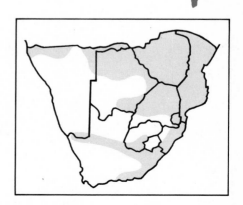

▲7♂

8 ▼

4 SAMANGO MONKEY *Cercopithecus mitis*
(Samango-aap)

Description: This scarce and little-known monkey has a conspicuously long tail. The shoulders, legs and large parts of the tail are black. The face is dark-brown and framed with lighter hair. The chest and belly are a dull-yellow colour. The rest of the body is light brown, darkening as the animal grows older. It differs from the Vervet Monkey by having a heavier build and a darker colour, especially on the legs. It is more closely associated with forests than the Vervet Monkey.

Sexual dimorphism: Males are larger than females.

Habitat: Mountain, riverine, dry and coastal forests.

Habits: Samango Monkeys are very shy diurnal animals spending most of their time in trees. They form troops of 4–30 animals, consisting of one or more adult males, the rest being females and young. They sleep at night and rest in the heat of the day high in trees in thick foliage. In the morning they bask in the sun for a while before going out to forage. Foraging is alternated with resting periods. They are not very aggressive – but generally their heads are pushed forward and the eyebrows raised to muster an aggressive expression designed to keep an inferior in his place.

Voice: A high birdlike noise or a "njah" alarm call. Females and young scream and chatter.

Food: Mostly wild fruit as well as flowers, leaves, and insects.

Gestation period: ± 4 months.

Breeding: September – April.

Number of young: One.

Mass: ♂ 8,2 – 10,0 kg (18 – 22 lb).
♀ 4,5 – 5,2 kg (10 – 12 lb).

Shoulder height: ♂ ± 39 cm (± 15″).
♀ ± 35 cm (± 13″).

Life expectancy: Unknown.

Tail: ± 80 cm (± 31″).

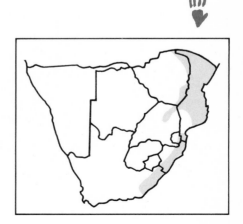

▲9 ♂

10 ♀▼

5 BAT-EARED FOX *Otocyon megalotis*
(Bakoorvos)

Description: The colouring is a light brownish-grey with a lighter coloured belly. The throat and forehead are also a lighter brown-grey. The edges of the ears and the legs are black. The beautiful coat is fluffy. The bushy black tail and large ears are characteristic. As it is not a jackal it is correctly named the Bat-eared Fox and can be distinguished from the Cape Fox by having larger ears and by the fact that it does not have the Cape Fox's silvery sheen.

Sexual dimorphism: Females are slightly heavier than males.

Habitat: Open areas in dry savannah or semi-arid areas.

Habits: Bat-eared Foxes are found either in pairs or in family groups with a maximum of 6 members. They are diurnal as well as nocturnal animals. During the hottest part of the day they rest in cool places such as old Antbear holes or holes which they dig. The hearing and scent is very keen and they are able to find insect larvae even underground, due to their keen hearing. Contrary to popular belief, they do not prey on sheep or lambs.

Voice: A "who-who" sound, or a shrill chattering alarm call by the young.

Food: Mainly insects and they also eat scorpions, termites, reptiles, mice and fruit.

Gestation period: ± 2 months.

Breeding: September – November.

Number of young: 2 – 6.

Mass: ♂ 3,4 – 4,9 kg (7 – 11 lb).
♀ 3,2 – 5,3 kg (7 – 12 lb).

Shoulder height: ± 30 cm (± 12″).

Life expectancy: ± 12 years.

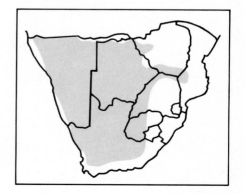

▲11   12▼

6 **WILD DOG** *Lycaon pictus*
(Wildehond)

Description: The animal has a short dark snout, large round ears and fairly long hair. A typical characteristic is the long white tail. The colour of the body and legs is white with blotches of yellow, brown and black. The colour pattern differs from animal to animal. The hair between the eyes and the ears is of a lighter colour with a dark stripe down the centre of the forehead, running backwards over the head.

Sexual dimorphism: None.

Habitat: Open areas and plains in woodland.

Habits: Wild Dogs live in packs of about 10–15 animals while larger packs of 40 or more animals are also known. They are mainly diurnal and are active during the early mornings and late afternoons when they range over large areas in their hunt for food. Spotted Hyaenas sometimes try to share their food. This usually results in the hyaenas being bullied when they get too forward. The young eat food regurgitated by the adults.

Hunting habits: The Wild Dog is more dependent on its eyesight than on its sense of smell. They hunt in groups chasing their prey until it is exhausted and eventually torn apart.

Voice: Excited "chirping" noises, a barking-growl or a "huu-huuu".

Food: Most types of antelope, especially Impala, Springbok and also Blue Wildebeest.

Gestation period: ± 2½ months.

Breeding: March – July.

Number of young: 7 – 10, very seldom up to 19.

Mass: 20 – 32 kg (44 – 70 lb).

Shoulder height: ± 68 cm (± 26″).

Life expectancy: ± 10 jaar.

14 ▼

7 CAPE FOX *Vulpes chama*
(Silwervos)

Description: The coat appears to be silver-grey at close range, but grey at a distance. On the upper front legs the colour is reddish-brown and there are dark brown patches on the buttocks. The head is reddish-brown and the cheeks white, the throat is dull yellow and the belly white with a ruddy sheen. The tail is darker, long and bushy. It is the only true fox in Southern Africa. It is smaller than the Bat-eared Fox and the ears are not as large.

Sexual dimorphism: Males are slightly heavier than females.

Habitat: Open plains with or without shrubs, open dry areas with trees, Karoo bushveld and fynbos.

Habits: The Cape Fox is mainly nocturnal and solitary. It is most active just after sunset and just before sunrise. During the day it sleeps in a hole in the ground or in the shelter of tall grass. It defends a small area around its den when raising young. The Cape Fox is a strong digger and digs its own burrow or simply adapts an old Springhare hole. It is a skilled mice hunter but, contrary to popular belief, does not prey on sheep or lambs.

Voice: A high howling bark.

Food: Mice and insects as well as reptiles, spiders and birds.

Gestation period: ± 2 months.

Breeding: October – November.

Number of young: 1 – 5.

Mass: ♂ ± 2,8 kg (± 6 lb).
♀ ± 2,5 kg (± 5,5 lb).

Shoulder height: ± 33 cm (± 13″).

Life expectancy: Unknown.

8 SIDE-STRIPED JACKAL *Canis adustus*
(Witkwasjakkals)

Description: The colour of this rather scarce jackal is grey or greyish-brown with a white stripe on the flanks below which is sometimes a dark stripe. The snout is dark and the belly, throat and inner parts of the legs a lighter colour, almost white. The tail is bushy, dark in colour with a white tip. The ears are upright and the tips are slightly rounded. It is distinguished from the Black-backed Jackal by not having the black saddle.

Sexual dimorphism: Females are slightly smaller than males.

Habitat: They prefer well watered terrain and are not found in arid country.

Habits: Side-striped Jackals are shy and seldom seen. They usually forage alone, but pairs and females with their young may be seen. They are mainly nocturnal and are also active in twilight. During the day they rest in old Antbear holes or other shelters. In moving they walk or trot slowly. They are scavengers, but may hunt small animals.

Voice: Series of pitiful yelps.

Food: Carrion, wild fruit, hares, moles and mice.

Gestation period: 2 – 2½ months.

Breeding: August – January.

Number of young: 2 – 6.

Mass: ♂ 7,3 – 12,0 kg (16 – 26 lb).
♀ 7,3 – 10,0 kg (16 – 22 lb).

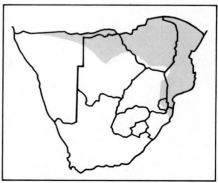

Shoulder height: ± 39 cm (± 15″).

Life expectancy: ± 11 years.

▲ 17 ♂

18 ♀ ▼

9 BLACK-BACKED JACKAL
Canis mesomelas
(Rooijakkals)

Description: The colour of the body and legs is reddish-brown to orange-brown. The throat, underparts and insides of the legs are whitish. The most outstanding feature being the black saddle on the back which is broad on the shoulders and narrow towards the bushy black tail. The ears are upright and more pointed at the tips than those of the Side-striped Jackal which lacks the black saddle and the Black-backed Jackal lacks the white stripes on the flanks and the white tip to the tail.

Sexual dimorphism: Males are slightly larger than females.

Habitat: They occur in most habitats, even in the most arid areas.

Habits: Sometimes seen in pairs, Black-blacked Jackal generally hunt and feed alone. They are diurnal and nocturnal and are usually seen towards sunrise or sunset and in the early hours of the night. They are cunning and shy and have an acute sense of smell. They usually move at a quick trot. They are scavengers, as well as hunters of small animals and birds, and are able to exist for long periods without water. During the day they rest in old Antbear holes or other shelters. Black-backed Jackal still occur outside conservation areas and are more common than Side-striped Jackal.

Voice: A long frightening "njaaaa" and a "na-ha-ha-ha" sound.

Food: Carrion, small mammals, birds, insects and wild fruit.

Gestation period: ± 2 months.

Breeding: July – October.

Number of young: 1 – 6, exceptional 9.

Mass: ♂ 6,8 – 11,4 kg (15 – 25 lb).
♀ 5,5 – 10,0 kg (12 – 22 lb).

Shoulder height: ± 38 cm (± 14″).

Life expectancy: ± 13 years.

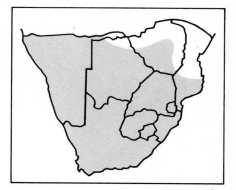

10 CAPE CLAWLESS OTTER
Aonyx capensis
(Groototter)

Description: The valuable coat consists of a dense covering of shiny protective hair. The upper parts of the body are brown, the rest slightly lighter in colour. The hindquarters are usually darker than the forequarters. The throat and sides of the face are white to below the ears and eyes. The toes of the hind feet are distinctly webbed. They can be distinguished from Spotted-necked Otters by the unspotted white area on the chest and throat going up to below the ears and eyes. They lack claws on the fore-feet and are larger than Spotted-necked Otters.

Sexual dimorphism: None.

Habitat: Usually in or near rivers, swamps, dams or lakes, but they sometimes wander far from water in search of new feeding grounds.

Habits: Usually solitary, but pairs and family groups are also seen. Mainly diurnal they are usually active in the early morning and late afternoon. They are sometimes active during the night. When it is hot they rest in dry shelters among rocks but most of the day is spent in the water and when emerging they shake their heads, and then their bodies, and slide on the ground to dry themselves. They are very playful animals and chase each other in the water.

Voice: High scream, a contented purring growl also hisses and growls when angry. Alarm call is an explosive "ha".

Food: Mainly frogs and crabs, but also fish, birds, insects and reptiles.

Gestation period: ± 9 weeks.

Breeding: Throughout the year.

Number of young: 1, seldom 2.

Mass: 10 – 18 kg (22 – 40 lb).

Length: ± 130 cm (± 51").

Life expectancy: ± 15 years.

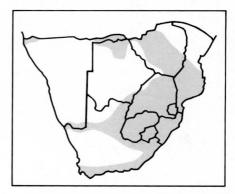

▲21

22▼

11 HONEY BADGER *Mellivora capensis*
(Ratel)

Also known as: Ratel.

Description: The body is black with a broad white, or brownish to greyish-white saddle on the head and back. It is a stocky animal with short legs, equipped with strong claws, ideal for digging. The hindquarters appear to be higher than the shoulders. The tail is short and black, the ears are very small. The skin is very thick and loose protecting it from the attacks of predators.

Sexual dimorphism: None.

Habitat: They are very adaptable and occur in most types of habitat, except deserts.

Habits: Honey Badgers are usually solitary, but two or three have been seen together. They usually rest during the heat of the day. Although they are mainly nocturnal, they are often seen during daytime. The walk is a rolling gait with their noses held close to the ground. They dig out spiders, scorpions, reptiles and bees. It is said that the Honey Guide bird leads the Honey Badger to bee-hives, waits until it has opened the bee-hive and then joins in feeding. They can be very aggressive and often fight other animals. When frightened they give off a sharp unpleasant odour like the Striped Polecat.

Voice: Growl, grunt, a high pitched bark and a nasal "harrrr-harrrrrr".

Food: Birds, fruit, scorpions, spiders and reptiles.
Honey and young bees are eaten with relish.

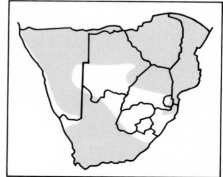

Gestation period: ± 6 months.

Breeding: October – January.

Number of young: Usually two.

Mass: 7,9 – 14,5 kg (17 – 32 lb).

Shoulder height: ± 26,5 cm (± 10″).

Life expectancy: ± 24 years.

12 STRIPED POLECAT *Ictonyx striatus*
(Stinkmuishond)

Description: A small black and white striped predator with short legs. The colour is black with four white stripes originating in a white patch on the head, stretching almost parallel along the back and flanks, to meet again at the base of the tail. There are white patches underneath the ears as well as on the forehead. The tail is thick and woolly with long black and white hair. It differs from the Snake Mongoose which has a smaller elongated body and lacks the white patches below the ears.

Sexual dimorphism: Males are larger than females.

Habitat: Found in all types of habitat – from desert-like areas with shrubs to forests.

Habits: Mainly solitary but sometimes occurring in pairs or females with their young. They are territorial, nocturnal animals becoming active late at night, and are very seldom seen during the day. They usually run with their backs humped. They make use of the old holes of other animals or take shelter under rock piles, or in rock clefts but do sometimes dig their own holes if the soil is soft. The nauseous exudation from the anal glands is used as a last resort in self-defence.

Voice: Growl and bark.

Food: Mainly insects and mice but they also eat reptiles, spiders, scorpions and millipedes.

Gestation period: 5 – 6 weeks.

Breeding: October – March.

Number of young: 1 – 3.

Mass: ♂ 681 – 1 460 g (1,5 – 3,2 lb).
♀ 596 – 880 g (1,3 – 2,0 lb).

Shoulder height: ± 10 cm (± 4″).

Life expectancy: ± 8 years.

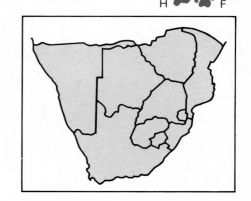

13 AFRICAN CIVET *Civettictis civetta*
(Afrikaanse siwet)

Description: The colour of this cat-like animal is whitish-grey with indistinct spots on the front quarters and regular black spots, which merge to stripes, on the hindquarters. There is a black stripe down the back starting from between the ears and extending to the base of the tail. The African Civet has a collar of white hair framed with black. The legs are black. The white tail is bushy and ringed with a black tip. The face is black with two white patches on either side of the nose, the ears rounded with white points.

Sexual dimorphism: Males are built slighter than females.

Habitat: Woodlands with thick undergrowth.

Habits: African Civet are exclusively nocturnal and are most active during the early night or just before sunrise, when they can sometimes be seen. They are mainly solitary foragers. They can climb trees but move mostly on the ground, usually using footpaths and walk purposefully with their heads down. They are very shy and when disturbed stand dead-still or lie down flat on the ground, depending on good camouflage rather than flight.

Voice: A low threatening growl and a coughing bark.

Food: Insects, mice, wild fruit, reptiles and birds.

Gestation period: ± 2 months.

Breeding: August – December.

Number of young: 1 – 4.

Mass: ♂ 9,5 – 13,2 kg (21 – 29 lb).
♀ 9,7 – 20,0 kg (21 – 44 lb).

Shoulder height: ± 40 cm (± 15″).

Life expectancy: ± 12 years.

H   F

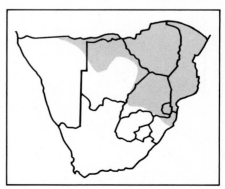

14 LARGE-SPOTTED GENET
Genetta tigrina
(Rooikolmuskejaatkat)

Also known as: Rusty-spotted Genet.

Description: The colour of this rather small, catlike animal is white or greyish-white with spots and stripes varying in colour from black to rust-brown. The tail is long and black or rust-brown with white rings. From just behind the shoulders to the base of the tail there is a distinct band of dark hair. Below the eyes are white spots and the cheeks are also white. These two white areas are divided by dark brown stripes from the corners of the eyes. The rounded ears stand upright. It can be distinguished from the Small-spotted Genet because the tip of its tail is black and the chin is white.

Sexual dimorphism: None.

Habitat: They prefer well watered areas with sufficient undergrowth.

Habits: Large-spotted Genets are usually solitary but are sometimes found in pairs. They are nocturnal, first appearing only a few hours after sunset. During the day they sleep in old Antbear or Springhare holes or in hollow tree stumps. They are mainly terrestrial but sometimes hunt in trees which they also use for shelter. They are skilful at jumping from one tree to another. Their movements are watchful and furtive and they run rapidly with their heads down and tails horizontal.

Voice: Growl and spit.

Food: Rats, mice, locusts, beetles, birds and sometimes crabs.

Gestation period: ± 2 months.

Breeding: August – March.

Number of young: 2 – 5.

Mass: 1,4 – 3,2 kg (3 – 7 lb).

Shoulder height: ± 15 cm (± 6″).

Life expectancy: ± 13 years.

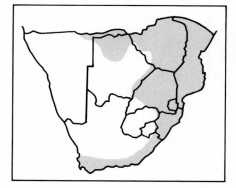

15 **SURICATE** *Suricata suricatta*
(Stokstertmeerkat)

Description: The colour is silver-brown, sometimes slightly paler. Darker spots, which become more obvious from the shoulders backwards, can be seen on their backs, these sometimes forming crosslines. The dark pointed tail is characteristic. It has a broad head and a dark area around the eyes. A fine dark stripe runs from above the eyes to the top of the ears. The hindquarters are heavier in build than the forequarters.

Sexual dimorphism: None.

Habitat: Open areas on hard calcareous or stony soil.

Habits: Suricates are playful, diurnal animals only appearing from their holes after sunrise, when they usually sit for quite a while with their bellies towards the sun. They live in colonies of up to 20 animals and use old burrows of Ground Squirrels, or dig their own with many tunnels, corridors and entrances. A typical posture is standing on their hind legs or sitting upright to watch the surroundings. When not playing, they are usually busy digging or turning over stones in search of food.

Voice: A sharp loud alarm bark.

Food: Worms, insects, larvae, mice and snake's eggs.

Gestation period: 10 – 11 weeks.

Breeding: October – March.

Number of young: 2 – 5.

Mass: 620 – 960 g (1,3 – 2,1 lb).

Length: ± 50 cm (± 20").

Life expectancy: ± 12 years.

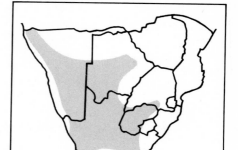

▲31

32▼

16 YELLOW MONGOOSE
Cynictus penicillata
(Witkwasmuishond)

Description: Over most of its range the Yellow Mongoose's colour is yellowish-brown or slightly yellowish-red with a white tip to the tail. The animals of the northern parts of Botswana are grey with speckles and the white tip to the tail is lacking. They are also much smaller with shorter hair and tails. The legs, chin, chest and throat of the Yellow Mongoose is slightly lighter in colour than the rest of the body. The Slender Mongoose is sometimes a yellow colour and always has a black-tipped tail.

Sexual dimorphism: None.

Habitat: Open grassy plains usually avoiding bushy areas.

Habits: They are gregarious animals and are found in colonies of 20 and more animals. The Botswana colonies are usually smaller. They often live socially with Ground Squirrels and Suricates but also dig their own burrows. These consist of many tunnels, corridors and entrances. They are mainly diurnal but are sometimes active after dusk. They forage far away from their dwelling holes and, if danger threatens, they make use of any shelter available.

Voice: Unknown.

Food: Beetles, termites, crickets, locusts, mice, birds and reptiles.

Gestation period: ± 8 weeks.

Breeding: October – March.

Number of young: 2 – 5.

Mass: 440 – 900 g (1 – 2 lb).

Length: ± 55 cm (± 22″).

Life expectancy: ± 12 years.

17 WATER MONGOOSE
Atilax paludinosus
(Kommetjiegatmuishond)

Also known as: Marsh Mongoose.

Description: A rather large mongoose. The colour of the body varies from almost black to rusty-brown and is sometimes speckled. The colour of the underparts, the head and the face is the same as the rest of the body, the legs are darker and are sometimes lighter on the chins. The hair is long, especially on the tail. The head is big and broad and the small ears lie flat. The Water Mongoose differs from the White-tailed Mongoose which is larger, darker in colour and has a white tail.

Sexual dimorphism: None.

Habitat: Always near rivers, streams, marshes, swamps and dams.

Habits: A solitary animal except when the female has young which follow her. It is active from dawn till mid-morning and again in the late-afternoon till dusk. It is active for a longer period on overcast days, sleeps in thick shelter and prefers footpaths or the muddy sides of streams or dams when foraging. It is an excellent swimmer, sometimes taking to water when threatened.

Voice: Growl and a high pitched explosive bark.

Food: Frogs, spur-toed frogs, crabs, mice, fish and insects.

Gestation period: Unknown.

Breeding: ± August – December.

Number of young: 1 – 3.

Mass: 2,4 – 4,1 kg (5,2 – 9 lb).

Shoulder height: ± 15 cm (± 6″).

Life expectancy: ± 11 years.

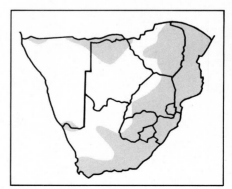

▲35

36▼

18 BANDED MONGOOSE *Mungos mungo*
(Gebande muishond)

Description: A small mongoose with colour varying from light-grey to reddish-brown with speckles. The colour of the limbs is the same as the rest of the body. The dark cross bands start in the centre of the back and end on the croup. The bands as well as the tip of the tail differs from black in dark coloured animals to brown in light coloured animals. It has small round ears and a pointed snout.

Sexual dimorphism: None.

Habitat: Riverine forest and dense *Acacia* woodland with sufficient undergrowth, fallen logs and other dry plant material.

Habits: Gregarious animals which live in colonies of 30 or more. They forage individually but keep contact by a continuous twittering. When in danger, or on hearing an alarm call, they all keep quiet, some will stand on their hind legs to keep watch on their surroundings. They will then quietly run away and seek temporary shelter in holes or will continue to feed. They are diurnal and during the night they sleep in holes in hollow antheaps. They can climb trees but usually move on the ground.

Voice: Twitter or a loud chittering noise used as an alarm call.

Food: Insects, snails, reptiles, worms, bird eggs, fruit and locusts.

Gestation period: ± 8 weeks.

Breeding: October – February.

Number of young: 2 – 8.

Mass: 1,0 – 1,6 kg (2,2 – 3,5 lb).

Shoulder height: ± 12,5 cm (± 5″).

Life expectancy: ± 8 years.

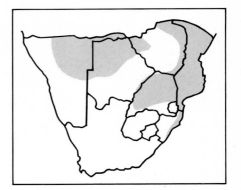

19 DWARF MONGOOSE *Helogale parvula*
(Dwergmuishond)

Description: This is the smallest of all the mongooses in the region. From a distance it appears to be dark brown but on closer examination the colour is dark brown with fine light speckles. The hair is sparser underneath the belly but of the same colour. The ears are small but, because of the very short hair on the head, are more prominent than those of any other mongoose. The claws on the fore-legs are long and well developed for digging.

Sexual dimorphism: None.

Habitat: In dry woodland with hard stony ground and where there are anthills, fallen logs and other detritus.

Habits: Gregarious animals living in colonies of 10 or more. Such a colony inhabits a permanent shelter which is either an old anthill or a hole dug by themselves with the entrance usually under an old log. They are diurnal, appearing only long after sunrise returning again before sunset. They are terrestrial and feed far apart but keep contact by "chook" noises. When the alarm call is given they all stiffen and some will stand on their hindlegs to search for the source of danger. They are fond of lying in the sun.

Voice: "Perrip" or "chook", or an alarm "shu-shwe".

Food: Termites, worms, snails, scorpions, locusts, earthworms, bird eggs and reptiles.

H   F

Gestation period: ± 8 weeks.

Breeding: October – March.

Number of young: 2 – 4.

Mass: 210 – 340 g (7 – 12 oz).

Shoulder height: ± 7,5 cm (± 3").

Life expectancy: ± 6 years.

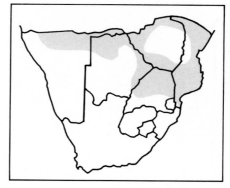

20 AARDWOLF *Proteles cristatus*
(Aardwolf)

Description: The colour of the body varies from yellow-brown to dull yellow, with ± 5 distinct vertical black stripes on the flanks and some on the legs. It has a long dark tipped mane on the back which bristles when the animal is frightened. The snout and lower parts of the legs are black. The ears are upright and pointed. The tail is bushy with a black tip. It is smaller than both the hyaenas, with a lighter colour than the Brown Hyaena, and without the spots of the Spotted Hyaena.

Differences between sexes: None.

Habitat: Dry open country, grassplains and dry vleis.

Habits: Aardwolfs are usually solitary but pairs and family groups are also seen. They are nocturnal animals which hide themselves in old Antbear holes or holes which they dig themselves and in which they rest during the day. Aardwolfs are neither carnivores nor scavengers and are sometimes wrongly identified as hyaenas. They have an acute sense of sight and of hearing. Aardwolf's defence consists of sometimes using their long canine teeth or lifting their manes, which makes them look much bigger especially in the dark. Under stress they have a very loud roar for their size.

Voice: A loud roar and a growl followed by a short bark.

Food: Mainly termites and other insects.

Gestation period: ± 2 months.

Breeding: September – April.

Number of young: 2 – 4.

Mass: 7,7 – 13,5 kg (17 – 30 lb).

Shoulder height: ± 50 cm (± 19″).

Life expectancy: ± 13 years.

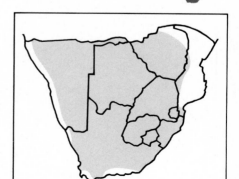

21 BROWN HYAENA *Hyaena brunnea*
(Bruinhiëna)

Description: The colour is dark brown with a light yellow-brown "cloak" on the shoulder and neck. The forehead and belly are of a dirty white colour. The hair is long and thick. The forequarters are stronger developed than the hindquarters, the back sloping downwards. The head is big and the ears pointed. It differs from the lighter coloured Spotted Hyaena, in having long hair, pointed ears and no spots. It is much larger and of a darker colour than the Aardwolf.

Sexual dimorphism: Females are smaller than males.

Habitat: Open dry woodland or open shrubby areas.

Habits: Brown Hyaena are gregarious, but some males are solitary. They usually forage alone ranging over large areas. They are shy, mainly nocturnal animals but are also seen in the early mornings and late afternoons. During the day they rest under thick bushes or in holes. They are scavangers and, in contrast with Spotted Hyaenas, seldom hunt larger animals. They are strong diggers and dig their own shelters or make use of old Antbear holes.

Voice: Yelp, snort and growl.

Food: Mainly carrion, but also birds, reptiles and small mammals.

Gestation period: ± 3 months.

Breeding: August – November.

Number of young: 2 – 5.

Mass: ♂   35 – 57 kg (77 – 125 lb).
♀   28 – 48 kg (62 – 106 lb).

Shoulder height: ♂ ± 79 cm (± 31″).
♀ ± 76 cm (± 30″).

Life expectancy: ± 24 years.

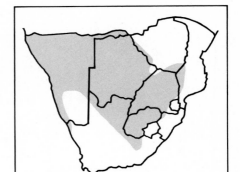

▲ 43 ♂   44 ♀ ▼

22 SPOTTED HYAENA *Crocuta crocuta*
(Gevlekte hiëna)

Also known as: Laughing Hyaena.

Description: The colour of the Spotted Hyaena is a dull yellow to white, with irregular dark brown spots. the snout and the lower parts of the legs are dark brown. The young are dark brown to black. It has a strong neck and forequarters and a sloping back. The front paws are larger than the hind paws. It has a big broad head with round ears. It is distinguished from the Brown Hyaena by the spots, round ears and shorter hair. The Aardwolf is smaller and has stripes and no spots.

Sexual dimorphism: Females are slightly larger than males.

Habitat: Savannah, open plains and woodland where there is sufficient game.

Habits: Spotted Hyaena are gregarious, forming groups, with a dominant female. Groups are usually small, although up to 11 animals have been seen together. They are frequently seen alone, or two or three together. Mainly nocturnal they are also seen in the early mornings or late afternoons. Their sense of smell, hearing and sight are acute. Spotted Hyaena are mainly scavengers but they also hunt in groups by chasing their prey till it is exhausted. As a group they sometimes try to drive Lion and Cheetah away from a kill.

Voice: A very typical sound of the African night: the "whooo-hoop" which starts low and ends high. Otherwise they make fearsome shouts and high pitched laughing sounds.

Food: Any type of carrion from fresh meat to skins and bones.

Gestation period: ± 3½ months.

Breeding: Throughout the year, with a peak in February to March.

Number of young: 1 – 4.

Mass: ♂ 46 – 79 kg (101 – 174 lb).
♀ 56 – 80 kg (123 – 176 lb).

Shoulder height: ± 77 cm (± 30").

Life expectancy: ± 25 years.

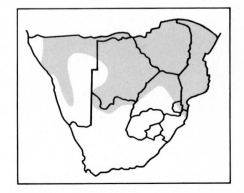

23 CHEETAH *Acinonyx jubatus*
(Jagluiperd)

Description: An elegant, slender cat with long legs. The colour is greyish-white with black spots. The belly, chin and throat are white, with smaller black spots on the chest. The spots on the tail are replaced by black rings toward the end. The ears are small, round and far apart. It is distinguished from the Leopard by longer legs, black spots on the body and the characteristic "tear" marks from the eyes to the mouth.

Sexual dimorphism: Females are slighter built than males.

Habitat: Open woodland and savannah.

Habits: Cheetahs are usually found in pairs, although individuals, small groups, or females with their young, have been seen. They are diurnal and most active at sunrise and sunset. During the hottest part of the day they rest in the shade of a tree. Cheetahs are the fastest of all animals, reaching a speed of 100 km/h and more over short distances. They are not aggressive although they sometimes paw and bite at each other.

Hunting habits: Usually hunt alone, except when they hunt larger animals, relying on speed to overtake their prey.

Voice: A high bird-like whistle.

Food: Ostriches, small to medium size antelope, warthogs, hares and guinea fowl.

Gestation period: ± 3 months.

Breeding: Throughout the year.

Number of young: 1 – 5.

Mass: ♂ 39 – 60 kg (86 – 132 lb).
♀ 36 – 48 kg (80 – 105 lb).

Shoulder height: ± 86 cm (± 34″).

Life expectancy: ± 12 years.

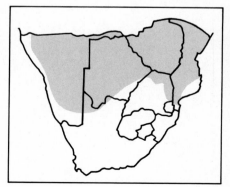

▲47

48▼

24 LEOPARD *Panthera pardus*
(Luiperd)

Description: The colouring of the Leopard varies from white to bright golden-brown, spotted with black spots and rosettes. The rosettes consist of groups of 5–6 spots arranged in a tight ring. The tail is longer than half the body length measured from head to tail. This cat has small round ears and long whiskers growing from dark spots on the upper lip. The size of the Leopard varies considerably in this region. It differs from the Cheetah in having shorter legs, and rosette-like spots. It is also without the Cheetah's black "tear" marks from eye to mouth.

Sexual dimorphism: Females are smaller than males.

Habitat: Mostly in or near thickets on mountain sides, along streams and rivers.

Habits: Leopards are mainly nocturnal animals but are also seen during the day, especially in the early mornings and late afternoons. They usually forage alone except in the mating season. They are shy, cunning and dangerous, especially when wounded. Leopards are very good tree-climbers and can pull fairly large prey up a tree to protect it, during their absence, from other predators or scavengers in the vicinity. They return later to feed again. They still occur outside conservation areas.

Hunting habits: They stalk and pounce upon their prey, making use of stealth and cover in their approach.

Voice: The most common voice is a hoarse cough, but other sounds are also made.

Food: From small animals like dassies to medium size antelope.

Gestation period: ± 3 months.

Breeding: Throughout the year.

Number of young: 2 – 3, very seldom up to 6.

Mass: ♂ 20 – 82 kg (44 – 180 lb).
♀ 17 – 35 kg (37 – 77 lb).

Shoulder height: ± 65 cm (± 26″).

Life expectancy: ± 20 years.

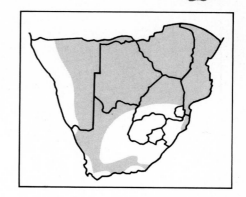

▲ 49 ♂ 50 ♀ ▼

25 LION *Panthera leo*
(Leeu)

Description: These tawny animals are the largest of Africa's cat family. The young have characteristic rosettes and spots which usually disappear as the animal matures. Males usually have manes, some being darker than others. The Lion has a white beard and long white whiskers growing from dark spots on the upper lip. The back of the ears is black, and the tail ends with a tuft of black hair. The large paws are padded, and have well developed claws.

Sexual dimorphism: Males are often maned and are larger than females.

Habitat: Lions are very adaptable and occur in most types of habitat where there is enough food.

Habits: Lions are the only social cats and form small prides of 3–12 animals; as many as 30 have been seen together. They are mainly nocturnal but are often seen during the day, especially at dawn and dusk. The pride consists of one, or occasionally more than one dominant male, a dominant female, mature and young animals. Lions generally sleep during the day.

Voice: The well-known "uuuuh-huumph" sound which starts high and then goes lower in tone, is repeated at intervals and becomes softer until it ends in a few groans.

Food: Carnivores which feed mainly on ungulates.

Gestation period: ± 3½ months.

Breeding: Throughout the year.

Number of young: 1 – 4, seldom up to 6.

Mass: ♂ 180 – 240 kg (396 – 530 lb).
♀ 120 – 180 kg (264 – 396 lb).

Shoulder height: ♂ ± 106 cm (± 42″).
♀ ± 91 cm (± 36″).

Life expectancy: ± 20 years.

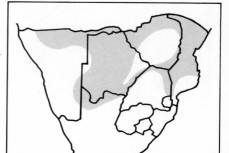

▲51♂

52♀▼

26 CARACAL *Felis caracal*
(Rooikat)

Also known as: Lynx.

Description: The Caracal is a well built animal with strong legs and remarkably big paws. The colour is light reddish-brown to brick-red, sometimes speckled with silver and the belly and chest are white. There are dark spots above and on the inner corners of the eyes and dark spots can also be seen at the base of the whiskers. It has black tassels of hair on the tips of the ears. The paws are dull yellow-white and the tail is fairly short. The size of the animal varies considerably in this region.

Sexual dimorphism: Females are slighter built than males.

Habitat: Most types of habitat particularly dry woodland or semi-arid areas.

Habits: Caracals are mainly nocturnal but can also be seen during daytime, especially in the early mornings and in the late afternoons, hunting alone. Although good tree-climbers, they are predominantly terrestrial. They rest during the hottest parts of the day, camouflaging themselves effectively even in little shelter.

Voice: Purr and "chirp" like a bird.

Food: Birds, small mammals and reptiles.

Gestation period: ± 2 months.

Breeding: October – March.

Number of young: 2 – 4, seldom 5.

Mass: ♂ 8,6 – 20,0 kg (19 – 44 lb).
♀ 4,2 – 14,5 kg (9 – 32 lb).

Shoulder height: ± 43 cm (± 17″).

Life expectancy: ± 11 years.

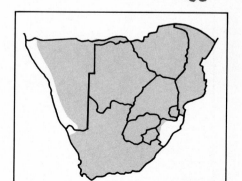

▲53 ♂

54 ♀▼

27 **SERVAL** *Felis serval*
(Tierboskat)

Description: The Serval is a slender built animal with long legs, a rather small rounded head and large ears. The colour varies from dull-white to light golden-yellow with black stripes against the neck and irregular black spots on the body. The tail is spotted from the base merging into black rings and ending in a black tip. The belly and the insides of the legs are white with dark spots. On the backs of the ears are two black stripes on white. It may be confused with a young Cheetah, but has larger ears and lacks the "tear" marks on the face of the Cheetah.

Sexual dimorphism: Females are slighter built than males.

Habitat: They prefer thicker, more humid types of woodland.

Habits: Servals usually forage alone although pairs sometimes hunt together, even in swampy areas. They are mainly nocturnal but can also be seen early in the morning and late in the afternoon. They can run very fast for short distances. At night they range far in search of food, using roads or footpaths to avoid difficult terrain. They are good tree-climbers, but are mainly terrestrial.

Voice: Repeated high-pitched call to partner. Snarls, growls and spits in anger.

Food: Small mammals like hares, mice, cane rats and sometimes birds.

Gestation period: ± 2 months.

Breeding: September – April.

Number of young: 1 – 4.

Mass: ♂ 8,6 – 13,5 kg (19 – 30 lb).
♀ 8,6 –11,8 kg (19 – 26 lb).

Shoulder height: ± 56 cm (± 22″).

Life expectancy: ± 12 years.

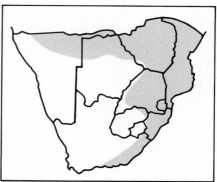

▲55

56▼

28 SMALL SPOTTED CAT *Felis nigripes*
(Klein gekolde kat)

Also known as: Black-footed Cat.

Description: The smallest cat in this region; the colour varies from cinnamon in the south to light yellow-brown in the north. The coat is marked with stripes and spots. On the back of the neck there are four black stripes, the outer two extending down over the shoulders. The stripes often break up into spots. There are three rings around the throat and the tail is short. It is distinguished from the African Wild Cat by being much smaller and lighter in colour and the spots and stripes more distinct.

Sexual dimorphism: Males are slightly heavier than females.

Habitat: Dry areas where there is enough open space as well as tall grass and shrubs for shelter.

Habits: Small Spotted Cats are very shy, nocturnal animals which only appear after dusk. They are very seldom seen during the day. They are usually solitary but are occasionally seen in pairs. They move and hunt on the ground, but are also good tree climbers. In wooded areas, like the Kalahari, they take to trees if they are threatened. During the day they sleep in old Antbear or Springhare holes, in hollow antheaps or under shrubs. They are very aggressive for their size and are not as easily tamed as other wildcats.

Voice: Spit and growl.

Food: Mainly mice and spiders but also reptiles and insects.

Gestation period: ± 2 months.

Breeding: November – December.

Number of young: 1 – 3.

Mass: ♂ 1,5 – 1,7 kg (3,3 – 3,7 lb).
♀ 1,0 – 1,4 kg (2,2 – 3,1 lb).

Shoulder height: ± 25 cm (± 10″).

Life expectancy: Unknown.

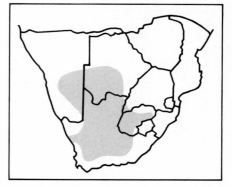

▲57

58▼

29 AFRICAN WILD CAT *Felis lybica*
(Vaalboskat)

Description: A slender built animal resembling the grey housecat. The colour varies from grey to dark grey with ± 6 reddish to blackish-red vertical stripes on the flanks and some on the legs. In some cases these stripes are very faint. The forehead is slightly darker while the throat and chest are lighter in colour, with a reddish tinge. The tail is darker than the body with a few lighter bands ending in black. It is larger and greyer in colour than the Small Spotted Cat.

Sexual dimorphism: Females are lighter in build than males.

Habitat: They are found everywhere, provided there is sufficient tall grass and rocks for shelter.

Habits: African Wild Cats are usually solitary, except during the mating season when one or more males are with a female. They are mainly nocturnal but can sometimes be seen late in the afternoon at sunset. They are territorial and both sexes will defend their areas. They are mainly ground-living but are good tree-climbers, especially when they are chased. They sometimes hunt in trees. African Wild Cats are shy and cunning animals.

Voice: Growl, hiss and purr.

Food: Usually mice, but also birds, insects and smaller mammals.

Gestation period: ± 2 months.

Breeding: Throughout the year, with a peak in the north of their distribution from September to March.

Number of young: 2 – 5.

Mass: ♂ 3,8 – 6,4 kg (8,4 – 14 lb).
♀ 2,6 – 5,5 kg (5,7 – 12,1 lb).

Shoulder height: ± 35 cm (± 14″).

Life expectancy: Unknown.

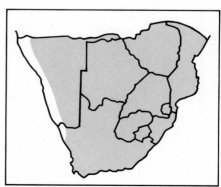

30 ELEPHANT *Loxodonta africana*
(Olifant)

Also known as: African Elephant.

Description: A huge heavily built animal with long stout legs and large feet. The colour is brownish-grey, sometimes similar to the ground colour of the vicinity in which it occurs. The skin is hairless but there is long hair on the end of the tail. This animal is characterised by large flat ears, a trunk and tusks varying in length. The trunk serves as a nose and is also used for breaking branches, for transferring all manner of vegetation to the mouth, and for siphoning up water for showering itself or for squirting into the mouth.

Sexual dimorphism: Females are smaller than males and have smaller tusks.

Habitat: Very adaptable, but they prefer areas providing grass and leafy vegetation.

Habits: Elephants are diurnal and nocturnal, forming herds of from 6 to ± 200 animals, with a cow as herd leader. Old males form small bachelor herds, but sometimes go solitary. They range widely in search of food. They are normally peaceful but can be dangerous, especially when they have calves or when wounded. Elephants are not fond of sharing drinking places with other animals, usually chasing them away. They swim well and enjoy wallowing in mud. They have a strong sense of smell, but hearing and sight are poor.

Voice: Trumpeting and a belly rumbling.

Food: Grass, leaves, branches, bark of trees and fruit.

Gestation period: ± 22 months.

Breeding: Throughout the year..

Number of young: Usually one, seldom two.

Mass: ♂ 5 500 – 6 000 kg (12 100 – 13 200 lb).
♀ 3 600 – 4 000 kg (7 920 – 8 800 lb).

Shoulder height: ± 350 cm (± 11′ 6″).

Life expectancy: ± 65 years.

Tusks: Record Mass: 102,7 kg (225,94 lb).
Record length: 3,48 m (11′5″).

H   F

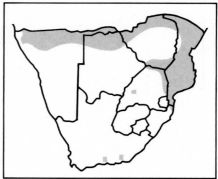

▲61♂

62♀▼

31 CAPE MOUNTAIN ZEBRA
Equus zebra zebra
(Kaapse bergkwagga)

Description: The body is white with black stripes. These stripes end in a horizontal line low down on the flanks, leaving the belly white. The stripes extend the full length of the legs to the hooves. Just behind the black nose is an orange suffusion. This zebra can be distinguished from the Burchell's Zebra by its dewlap and white belly. It has stripes right down to the hooves but lacks the shadow stripes of the Burchell's Zebra. The Hartmann's Mountain Zebra is heavier built and the stripes on the buttocks are usually narrower than those of the Cape Mountain Zebra.

Sexual dimorphism: Males are usually larger than females.

Habitat: Restricted to mountainous areas where water is available.

Habits: Cape Mountain Zebras are gregarious animals. Herds consist of a male, females and young animals. Other males are solitary or form bachelor herds. Members of the family group usually stay with the same herd for life. They are active early in the morning and in the late afternoon. They rest for the remainder of the day, not necessarily in the shade. They are very fond of a dust bath. If a young male challenges an older one, it leads to a fight in which they bite and kick each other.

Voice: A snort or a high-pitched alarm call if they are threatened.

Food: Grass and occasionally leaves.

Gestation period: ± 12 months.

Breeding: Throughout the year.

Number of young: One.

Mass: ♂ 250 – 260 kg (550 – 572 lb).
♀ 204 – 257 kg (449 – 565 lb).

Shoulder height: ♂ ± 127 cm (± 50″).
♀ ± 124 cm (± 49″).

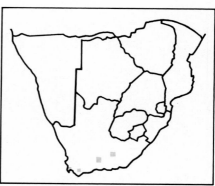

Life expectancy: ± 35 years.

32 HARTMANN'S MOUNTAIN ZEBRA

Equus zebra hartmannae
(Hartmannse bergkwagga)

Description: The black stripes of this zebra are clearly visible against the yellowish-white background. The legs are striped to the hooves. Some distance down the flanks the stripes end to leave the belly white. The dewlap as well as the orange suffusion above the snout are evident. It differs from the Burchell's Zebra by the absence of the shadow stripes, the presence of the dewlap and the white belly. It is heavier built than the Cape Mountain Zebra and the stripes on the buttocks are usually narrower.

Sexual dimorphism: Males are slightly heavier in build than females.

Habitat: Stony and mountainous areas.

Habits: Hartmann's Zebras are gregarious animals, forming herds which consist of a dominant male and his family-group. Other males form bachelor herds. The family group is stable and an individual will usually live his whole life in the same herd. They generally graze during the cooler parts of the day and rest in the shade during the hottest part of the day. They are very fond of dustbaths. Fights between males consist of biting and kicking.

Voice: Snorting and a shrill alarm call.

Food: Grass and occasionally small branches and shrubs.

Gestation period: ± 12 months.

Breeding: Throughout the year, with a peak in summer.

Number of young: One.

Mass: ♂   270 – 330 kg (594 – 726 lb).
♀   250 – 300 kg (550 – 660 lb).

Shoulder height: ± 150 cm (± 59″).

Life expectancy: ± 35 years.

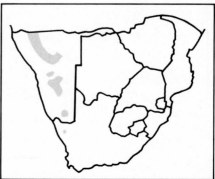

▲65

66▼

33 BURCHELL'S ZEBRA *Equus burchelli*
(Bontkwagga)

Description: This horse-like animal's body is white with dark stripes alternating with lighter shadow stripes. The pattern of these stripes differs in all animals. The colour of the stripes become less distinct towards the hooves. The Burchell's Zebra can be distinguished from the Mountain Zebra by having shadow stripes, a longer mane and smaller ears. It does not have a dewlap or a white belly.

Sexual dimorphism: Males are usually slightly heavier than females.

Habitat: Open savannah with grass and sufficient water.

Habits: Burchell's Zebras form family herds of 4–9 animals. These herds usually consist of a male, a few females and some young animals. They are diurnal animals which range over large areas in search of food. Their senses are acute and they enjoy a dust bath. Burchell's Zebras are often seen socially with Blue Wildebeest. A male will protect his herd, a female and her foal, by biting and kicking.

Voice: A repetitive "qua-ha-ha" whinny followed by a whistling sound as they inhale air.

Food: Grass, and occasionally leaves as well.

Gestation period: ± 12½ months.

Breeding: Throughout the year, with a peak in summer.

Number of young: One.

Mass: ♂ 290 – 340 kg (640 – 750 lb).
♀ 290 – 325 kg (640 – 715 lb).

Shoulder height: ± 134 cm (± 53″).

Life expectancy: ± 35 years.

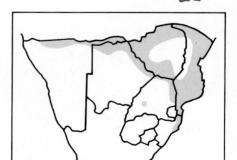

▲67 ♂

68 ♀▼

34 SQUARE-LIPPED RHINOCEROS

Ceratotherium simum
(Witrenoster)

Also known as: White Rhinoceros.

Description: The largest of the two rhinoceros. It is a prehistoric animal in appearance with a barrel shaped body and a long head with two horns on the snout. The horns are formed of tubular filament hair-like outgrowths, the front horn longer than the rear horn. The square lips are characteristic. The colour is grey but is sometimes similar to the ground colour of the vicinity in which it occurs. The ears are pointed. It is distinguished from the Hook-lipped Rhinoceros by the upper lip not being pointed. It is bigger, has a hump above the shoulders, and usually walks with the head closer to the ground.

Sexual dimorphism: Females are lighter in build than males.

Habitat: Open and bushy savannah with trees and thickets for cover.

Habits: They live in small groups consisting of a leader male, other males, females and juveniles. They are restricted to their home range, not wandering far afield. Although they appear clumsy, they can run surprisingly fast. Square-lipped Rhinoceros' calves usually walk in front of their mothers. Their eyesight is poor but they have an acute sense of smell and hearing. They are fond of wallowing in mud when it is hot and are not as aggressive as the Hook-lipped Rhinoceros.

Voice: Snort and growl.

Food: Grass, preferring short grass.

Gestation period: ± 16 months.

Breeding: Throughout the year.

Number of young: One.

Mass: ♂ 2 000 – 2 300 kg (4 400 – 5 060 lb).
♀ 1 400 – 1 600 kg (3 080 – 3 520 lb).

Shoulder height: ± 170 cm (± 5′ 7″).

Life expectancy: ± 45 years.

Record horn: 158 cm (5′2⅕″)

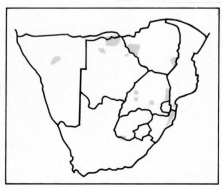

35 HOOK-LIPPED RHINOCEROS
Diceros bicornis
(Swartrenoster)

Also known as: Black Rhinoceros.

Description: The smallest of the rhinoceros. It has a barrel-shaped body and long head with two horns on the snout. The horns are formed of tubular filament hair-like outgrowths. The ears are small and rounded. The upper lip is pointed and prehensile. The colour is dark grey but is sometimes similar to the ground colour of the vicinity in which it occurs. It is distinguished from the Square-lipped Rhinoceros by the pointed upper lip, the shorter head and smaller build, and lacks the hump above the shoulders. When it walks it usually holds its head higher than does the Square-lipped Rhinoceros.

Sexual dimorphism: Males are slightly lighter in build than females.

Habitat: Dense shrubby and treed areas with plenty of water.

Habits: They are usually solitary or a cow and her calf together. The calves usually walk behind their mothers. they are fond of mudbaths and rest in shady areas when it is hot. The eyesight is poor but the senses of smell and hearing are acute. They browse early in the morning or late afternoon and drink water in the evening. Males avoid contact with each other and sometimes fight to the death. Hook-lipped Rhinoceros are sometimes moody and charge blindly, often just to ascertain if there is danger in the object.

Voice: Snorts which are repeated, they also growl and scream.

Food: Leaves, branches and thorns.

Gestation period: ± 15 months.

Breeding: Throughout the year.

Number of young: One.

Mass: ♂ 730 – 970 kg (1 600 – 2 130 lb).
♀ 760 – 1 000 kg (1 670 – 2 200 lb).

Shoulder height: ± 160 cm (± 5′ 3″).

Life expectancy: ± 40 years.

Record horn: 105 cm (41⅓′).

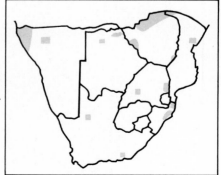

36 ROCK DASSIE *Procavia capensis*
(Klipdassie)

Description: This a a small stockily-built tailless animal. Its colour varies from grey-brown to ash-brown with a yellow or red tinge and fine black speckles. On the back is an oblong patch of black hair which in other species is white or yellow. The hair around the mouth, behind the ears, above the eyes, and on the underparts, is lighter in colour. The Yellow-spotted Rock Dassie's dorsal patch is yellow and it has white eyebrows while the Tree Dassie differs from both the previous species as the hair is longer and more woolly.

Sexual dimorphism: Males are slightly larger than females.

Habitat: Rocks, cliffs and stony hills with a covering of bushes and trees.

Habits: Rock dassies are hierarchial and are mainly diurnal animals living in colonies which may number from 4 to a few hundred. Few fights occur, but, when aggressive, they growl and show their teeth and the black hair on their back bristles. They prefer to forage in the early morning and late afternoon, and even after dusk when there is sufficient moonlight. On cold days they sit in the morning sun to warm themselves before they begin to feed. Rock Dassies are good tree-climbers.

Voice: A sharp alarm bark. But they also growl, snort, scream and chirp.

Food: Grass, shrubs and herbs.

Gestation period: ± 7½ months.

Breeding: In winter rainfall regions a peak in September to October and in summer rainfall regions a peak in March to April.

Number of young: 1 – 6.

Mass: ♂ 3,2 – 4,7 kg (7 – 10 lb).
♀ 2,5 – 4,2 kg (5,5 – 9,3 lb).

Shoulder height: ± 25 cm (± 10″).

Life expectancy: ± 6 years.

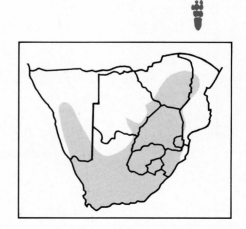

37 **ANTBEAR** *Orycteropus afer*
(Erdvark)

Also known as: Aardvark.

Description: An animal with long ears, a long pig-like snout and a thick tail. The skin is almost bare and of a yellow-grey colour but the hair against the legs is darker in colour. It also takes the colour of the soil of the area in which it lives. The hindquarters are much heavier than the forequarters with the shoulders lower than the croup. The limbs are powerful and the feet, especially the forefeet, are equipped with strong claws designed for digging and for breaking up anthills.

Sexual dimorphism: Males become slightly heavier in build than females.

Habitat: Most types of habitat found in this region.

Habits: Generally solitary, Antbears range widely seeking food, with their noses held close to the ground. They have a strong sense of hearing and smell, but have poor eyesight. They are mainly nocturnal and usually sleep during the daytime in a hole which they fill in behind them. They can dig at an unbelievable rate. Three kinds of holes can be distinguished: the first hole in which they live and in which the young are born; secondly a temporary shelter; and thirdly a small excavation for the purpose of searching for food. Their teeth are poorly developed and they use their sticky tongues to catch termites.

Voice: Snuffle and grunt.

Food: Chiefly termites and ants.

Gestation period: ± 7 months.

Breeding: July – September.

Number of young: One.

Mass: ♂ 41 – 65 kg (90 – 143 lb).
  ♀ 40 – 58 kg (88 – 128 lb).

Shoulder height: ± 61 cm (± 24″).

Life expectancy: ± 10 years.

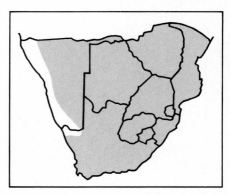

38 WARTHOG *Phacochoerus aethiopicus*
(Vlakvark)

Description: The Warthog has distinctive white whiskers and warts on the sides of the face. The grey body is sparsely covered with long bristles and there is a mane of dark hair with lighter tips. The tip of the tail has a small tuft of black hair. The adult has long tusks which curve over a broad snout. It is seen more often than the Bushpig from which it is distinguished by the broader snout, long curved tusks and more prominent warts on the face. It is grey, not dark brown like the Bushpig.

Sexual dimorphism: Males are large and have two pairs of warts and long tusks. The females' tusks are shorter and they have only one pair of warts.

Habitat: Savannah with open areas around pans and waterholes.

Habits: Warthogs are diurnal and form family or bachelor groups of 4–10 animals. They are sometimes solitary. They live in old Antbear holes entering backwards and emerging head first. They are able to defend themselves against Cheetahs and Wild Dogs, but are not strong enough to defend themselves against Lions. They are fond of digging in the soil or taking mudbaths and as they run they characteristically lift their tails upright like aerials. They kneel down on their front legs, when they root and graze..

Voice: Growl, grunt and snort.

Food: Grass and fallen wild druit such as maroelas. They also root for the succulent roots of grasses with their snouts.

Gestation period: ± 5½ months.

Breeding: September – December.

Number of young: 1 – 8.

Mass: ♂ 60 – 100 kg (132 – 220 lb).
♀ 45 – 70 kg (99 – 154 lb).

Shoulder height: ♂ ± 70 cm (± 27″).
♀ ± 60 cm (± 24″).

Life expectancy: ± 20 years.

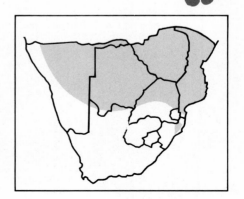

▲77 ♂

78♀▼

39 BUSHPIG *Potamochoerus porcus*
(Bosvark)

Description: A very hairy animal which resembles the domestic pig. The colour varies from grey-brown to dark brown, becoming darker as it ages. The mane, which bristles when the animal is under stress, is of a lighter colour. The upper parts of the face are lighter in colour and the lower portions of the legs are black. The sharp tusks are not very long. The young have distinct white horizontal stripes on the body. They are browner than the Warthog and usually lack the warts on the face and have smaller tusks, a narrower snout and more pointed ears.

Sexual dimorphism: Males are usually slightly larger than females.

Habitat: They frequent thickets, riverine underbush and reedbeds.

Habits: Bushpigs form groups of 6–12 animals consisting of a dominant male, a dominant female, other females and juveniles. They are nocturnal and are seldom seen during daytime as they usually rest in thick shelter. Small groups with young are always aggressive. Bushpigs are dangerous when wounded. They are good swimmers and like to wallow in cooling mud. Like Warthogs, they are fond of digging in the soil.

Voice: The alarm call is a long resonant growl and they grunt softly when foraging.

Food: They root in the ground for the underground rhizomes of grasses, bulbs and tubers and will eat green maize cobs, root vegetables, fieldpeas and beans.

Gestation period: ± 4 months.

Breeding: November – January.

Number of young: 3 – 8.

Mass: ♂ 46 – 82 kg (101 – 180 lb).
♀ 48 – 66 kg (105 – 145 lb).

Shoulder height: ± 75 cm (± 30″).

Life expectancy: ± 20 years.

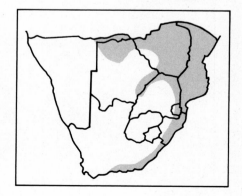

40 HIPPOPOTAMUS
Hippopotamus amphibius
(Seekoei)

Description: A very large, distinctive aquatic animal. The colour is grey-brown but the belly and skin folds are yellow-pink. The skin is virtually bare. It has short legs and is stockily built. The mouth is very large and the eyes are situated on top of the head. It usually lies submerged in the water with only the nose, eyes and ears protruding. The upright ears are small in relation to the head and the tail is short and flattened.

Sexual dimorphism: Males are larger than females.

Habitat: Stretches of open permanent water in which they can submerge and sandbanks.

Habits: These gregarious animals form schools of 6–15 members. They feed at night and rest during the day, half submerged in the water, or otherwise bask on sandbanks. In the late afternoon they begin to move out of the water to feed. Sometimes they feed several kilometres from water. They often use the same route, eventually trampling it into a wide path. Although they are generally placid animals they can be aggressive and even very dangerous at times, this is especially true of cows with calves.

Voice: A mixture between a loud high roar and a bellow, followed by ± 5 successive lower pitched short calls.

Food: Mainly grass. They can eat up to 130 kg each night.
They are also notorious crop raiders outside conservation areas.

Gestation period: 7½ – 8½ months.

Breeding: Throughout the year.

Number of young: One.

Mass: ♂ 970 – 2 000 kg (2 100 – 4 400 lb).
♀ 995 – 1 675 kg (2 190 – 3 685 lb).

Shoulder height: ♂ ± 150 cm (± 5′).
♀ ± 144 cm (± 4′ 9″).

Life expectancy: ± 39 years.

Record canine: 30,8 cm (12″).

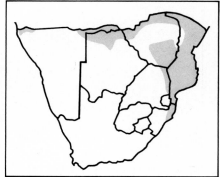

▲81 ♂

82 ♀▼

41 GIRAFFE *Giraffa camelopardalis*
(Kameelperd)

Description: This animal is characterised by a very long neck, which has seven cervical vertebrae – the same number as man. The background colour is whitish-yellow covered with patches of light brown which become darker with age. On top of the head are two short horns, the tops of which are covered with black hair. There are no dark patches on the upper part of the muzzle and on the forehead. They have a mane of short stiff hair.

Sexual dimorphism: Females are usually slighter built than males.

Habitat: Open woodland to shrubby dry savannah.

Habits: Giraffe are diurnal animals which live in herds with a fairly loose structure, individuals moving between the herds as they please. Males are usually solitary. They usually rest during the hottest part of the day. As they walk the legs on the same side swing simultaneously. Although they appear clumsy, they can gallop surprisingly fast. Females with calves defend themselves against Lion and can even kill them. Males fight by swinging and hitting each other with their necks and heads.

Voice: Grunt or snort, if alarmed.

Food: Mainly leaves but also grass.

Gestation period: ± 15 months.

Breeding: Throughout the year.

Number of young: One.

Mass: ♂ 970 – 1 395 kg (2 134 – 3 069 lb).
♀ 700 – 950 kg (1 540 – 2 090 lb).

Shoulder height: ± 300 cm (± 9′ 10″).

Life expectancy: ± 28 years.

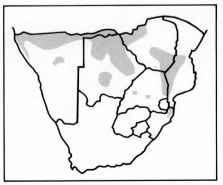

42 BLACK WILDEBEEST
Connochaetes gnou
(Swartwildebees)

Also known as: White-tailed Gnu.

Description: An ox-like animal with unusual horns, a beard and hair on the nose. The colouring is dark brown and the horse-like tail is almost white. The calves are a uniform light brown colour. The back slants downwards. Both sexes have horns. It can be distinguished from the Blue Wildebeest by its conspicious white tail, smaller build and horns which bend forward.

Sexual dimorphism: Females are smaller than males.

Habitat: Open grassland.

Habits: These animals occur naturally only in South Africa. They form herds of 6 – ± 50 individuals consisting of adult males, females and juveniles, or adult males only. They usually graze in the early morning or late afternoon. When it is cold they graze at any time. Sometimes they are seen kneeling while they feed. They rest during the hottest part of the day. Males are very aggressive during the mating season when they protect their territories and fights often occur.

Voice: A loud snorting bellow.

Food: Mainly grass and sometimes karoo bush.

Gestation period: ± 8½ months.

Breeding: November – December.

Number of young: One.

Mass: ♂ ± 180 kg (± 400 lb).
♀ ± 140 kg (± 300 lb).

Shoulder height: ♂ ± 120 cm (± 47″).
♀ ± 110 cm (± 43″).

Life expectancy: ± 20 years.

Record horns: 74,6 cm (29⅜″).

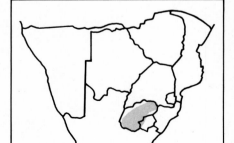

▲ 85 ♂

86 ▼

43 BLUE WILDEBEEST
Connochaetes taurinus
(Blouwildebees)

Also known as: Brindled Gnu.

Description: The colour of this ox-like animal is dark grey-brown with darker vertical stripes on the neck and flanks. The mane, beard, throat hairs and long horse-like tail are black. The calf is a light reddish-brown colour and has short upright horns. The back slants downwards. Both males and females have horns. It can be distinguished from the Black Wildebeest by its larger size and because it does not occur on the grass plains of the Transvaal and Orange Free State Highveld. The Black Wildebeest's horns bend forward and the tail is white.

Sexual dimorphism: Females are considerably smaller than males.

Habitat: Open bushveld with plenty of grass and water.

Habits: Blue Wildebeest are gregarious, diurnal animals. There are 20–30 animals in a herd which consists mainly of females and young, with a male as leader. Bachelor herds and very large herds also exist. They usually graze while it is cool and rest during the hottest part of the day, constantly moving about searching for good grazing. They often mingle socially with Burchell's Zebras. During mating season the males mark out a certain territory for themselves. Characteristically, they shake their heads, swing their tails, run away for a short distance and then look back.

Voice: Snort and bellow. Young ones bleat or make a "hunn" noise.

Food: Grass.

Gestation period: ± 8½ months.

Breeding: November – February.

Number of young: One, occasionally two.

Mass: ♂ 230 – 270 kg (506 – 600 lb).
♀ 160 – 200 kg (350 – 440 lb).

Shoulder height: ♂ ± 150 cm (± 60″).
♀ ± 135 cm (± 53″).

Life expectancy: ± 20 years.

Record horns: 84,14 cm (38⅛″).

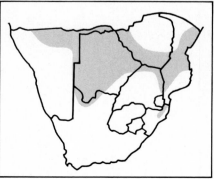

44 LICHTENSTEIN'S HARTEBEEST
Sigmoceros lichtensteinii
(Mofhartbees)

Description: The animal is coloured dull yellow-brown or chestnut with the buttocks around the tail a lighter colour. The tuft of hair on the tail, and the shins are black. The black patches, sometimes seen just behind the shoulders, are caused by the rubbing of the horns and sides of the face after it has horned the ground or grazed on burned tufts of grass. The shoulders are humped and both sexes are horned. It differs from the Red Hartebeest in its lighter colour, it does not have a black blaze on the face and lacks the high pedicel which carries the horns.

Sexual dimorphism: Females are slightly smaller than males.

Habitat: Areas between vleis and the surrounding woodland or dry floodplains.

Habits: Lichtenstein's Hartebeest form herds of 3–15 animals consisting of a dominant male, females and juveniles. Other males are solitary or form small herds. They rest during the hottest part of the day, and graze when it is cooler. They have acute sense of sight but poor sense of smell. The males stand on top of anthills to survey the vicinity for any threat, probably the main reason why they became extinct by hunting in South Africa. During 1985 they were reintroduced into the Kruger National Park.

Voice: Bellow or a sneezing snort.

Food: Grass, especially fresh sprouting green grass and sometimes leaves. They drink water regularly.

Gestation period: ± 8 months.

Breeding: June – September.

Number of young: One.

Mass: ♂ 157 – 204 kg (345 – 450 lb).
♀ 160 – 181 kg (350 – 400 lb).

Shoulder height: ♂ ± 129 cm (± 51″).
♀ ± 124 cm (± 49″).

Life expectancy: Unknown.

Record horns: 61,91 cm (24⅜).

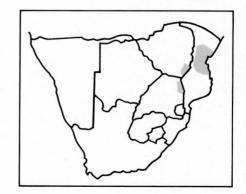

45 RED HARTEBEEST
Alcelaphus buselaphus
(Rooihartbees)

Also known as: Cape Hartebeest.

Description: This hartebeest has peculiarly shaped horns and a long face. The colour is a glossy reddish-brown. The blaze on the face, the tail and the outside of the legs is black, while the backside of the buttocks is light brown. The shoulders are high and humped and the back slants downwards. It can be distinguished from Lichtenstein's Hartebeest by the reddish-brown colouring, the black blaze on the face and the black legs. The horns of the Tsessebe have a different shape and their colouring is not as reddish-brown.

Sexual dimorphism: Females are smaller than males.

Habitat: Open areas or grassplains in dry savannah and semi-arid areas.

Habits: Red Hartebeest are animals which form herds of 10–30 animals or in some cases up to a few hundred. Old males are solitary or form small herds. Other herds consist of females, and young with a male as leader. They usually graze early in the morning and late in the afternoon. They have acute senses of smell and hearing but their eyesight is poor. They can run very fast with a graceful gallop. They are very inquisitive, running a short distance, stopping and looking back and may even approach closer again.

Voice: A warning sneezing-snort.

Food: Exclusively grass. They can survive for long periods without water.

Gestation period: ± 8 months.

Breeding: October – December.

Number of young: One.

Mass: ♂ 137 – 180 kg (301 – 396 lb).
♀ 105 – 136 kg (231 – 300 lb).

Shoulder height: ± 125 cm (± 49″).

Life expectancy: ± 13 years.

Record horns: 74,93 cm (29½″).

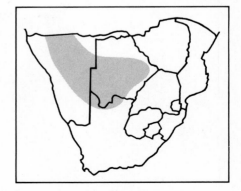

▲91 ♂

92 ♀▼

46 **BONTEBOK** *Damaliscus dorcas dorcas*
(Bontebok)

Description: This is a colourful animal with the brown in some places shading to dark-brown and black with a purple sheen. The belly, the area inside of the buttocks, a patch around the croup and down on the lower legs are white. Both sexes have horns and the small blaze above the eyes and the big blaze usually merge. It can be distinguished from the Blesbok by the larger white patches on the body, especially the white patch around the croup.

Sexual dimorphism: Females are slightly smaller than males.

Habitat: Open grassplains in fynbos.

Habits: Bontebok form herds of separate sexes. Some males are territorial and are solitary. If a female herd passes through his area in the mating season, he will round them up and court them. Territorial males use the same manure heap and sometimes lie down on top of it. They usually graze early in the morning and late in the afternoon and rest during the hottest part of the day. They were an endangered species but their survival is now assured in the Bontebok Park near Swellendam from where the translocation of surplus stock to other areas is now possible.

Voice: Growl and snort.

Food: Exclusively grass.

Gestation period: ± 8 months.

Breeding: September – November.

Number of young: One.

Mass: 59 – 64 kg (130 – 140 lb).

Shoulder height: ± 90 cm (± 35″).

Life expectancy: ± 11 years.

Record horns: 43,18 cm (17″).

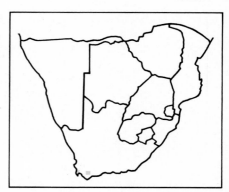

47 BLESBOK *Damaliscus dorcas phillipsi*
(Blesbok)

Description: The neck and top of the back is brown. Lower down on the flanks and buttocks the colouring becomes darker. The belly, the inside of the buttocks and up to the base of the tail is white. The small blaze above the eyes and the big blaze are usually divided between the eyes. The lambs are a much lighter brown. Both sexes have horns. It differs from the Bontebok by having less white on the coat and the blaze on the face is usually divided.

Sexual dimorphism: Females are slighter in build than males.

Habitat: Open plains of the South African highveld..

Habits: Blesbok form herds consisting of females and juveniles. Males are solitary. They graze in the morning and late in the afternoon and rest during the hottest part of the day. During mating season the males collect a herd of females which pass through their areas and court them. During mating season serious fights occur between the males. Sometimes the males lie on heaps of manure to rest. Blesbok have the habit of walking in single file.

Voice: Snort and growl.

Food: Exclusively grass.

Gestation period: ± 8 months.

Breeding: November – January.

Number of young: One.

Mass: ♂ ± 70 kg (± 155 lb).
♀ ± 61 kg (± 135 lb).

Shoulder height: ± 95 cm (± 37″).

Life expectancy: ± 11 years.

Record horns: 50,8 cm (20″).

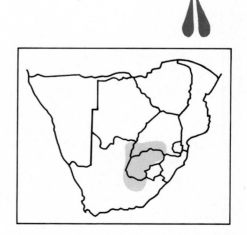

48 TSESSEBE *Damaliscus lunatus*
(Basterhartbees)

Also known as: Sassaby.

Description: The colouring is dark reddish-brown with a metallic sheen. The blaze on the face as well as the upper parts of the fore and hind legs down to the knees are black. Below the knees the colour is light brown. It has a hump on the shoulders and the back slopes characteristically downwards. Both sexes have horns. It differs from the Red Hartebeest because its colour is not as red and the horns are shorter and spaced more widely apart, while the face of the Lichtenstein's Hartebeest lacks the black blaze of the Tsessebe.

Sexual dimorphism: Females are smaller than males.

Habitat: Open savannah and grassplains in surrounding woodland.

Habits: Tsessebe are gregarious and are usually found in small breeding herds, bachelor groups or family herds with a dominant male. During the winter they herd together more often. They are very inquisitive and usually run away for only a short distance and then stop and look back. Tsessebe are the fastest of all the region's antelope. They are fond of horning the ground, especially after rain. They are sometimes found together with Zebra or Blue Wildebeest.

Voice: Snort.

Food: Exclusively grass and they are dependent on water.

Gestation period: ± 8 months.

Breeding: September – November.

Number of young: One.

Mass: ♂ 140 kg (± 308 lb).
♀ 126 kg (± 280 lb).

Shoulder height: ♂ ± 126 cm (± 50″).
♀ ± 125 cm (± 49″).

Life expectancy: ± 15 years.

Record horns: 46,99 cm (18½″).

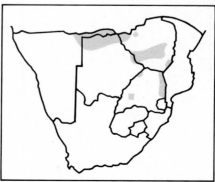

▲ 97 ♂   98 ♀ ▼

49 BLUE DUIKER *Philantomba monticola*
(Blouduiker)

Description: The Blue Duiker is our smallest antelope. The colour varies from dark reddish-brown to dark greyish-brown and is darker on the back with a blueish sheen. Colouring is lighter on the belly and against the throat and chest. The cheeks and areas around the eyes are light-brown in colour with two horizontal black stripes from below the eyes towards the nose. The tail is white underneath and has a white edge. Both sexes have short horns which slope backwards, in the line of the face.

Sexual dimorphism: Males are slightly lighter in build than females.

Habitat: Limited to forests, thickets and coastal bush.

Habits: Blue Duiker are usually solitary but are also found in pairs. They are very shy and will, at the slightest disturbance, flee to shelter in the thick undergrowth. They usually browse in the early morning or late afternoon and even at night. During the night they come out to the more open areas on the edge of the forest. During the day they are always alert and approach open spots with great care.

Voice: A sharp alarm whistle.

Food: Mainly leaves, but also fruit and young branches.

Gestation period: ± 4 months.

Breeding: Throughout the year.

Number of young: One.

Mass: ♂ 3,8 – 5,5 kg (8 – 12 lb).
♀ 4,6 – 7,3 kg (10 – 16 lb).

Shoulder height: ± 30 cm (± 12″).

Life expectancy: ± 7 years.

Record horns: 9,84 cm (3⅘″).

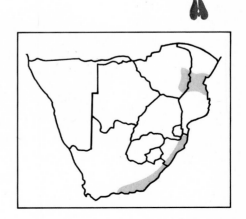

50 RED DUIKER *Cephalophus natalensis*
(Rooiduiker)

Also known as: Natal Duiker.

Description: The colour is chestnut to reddish-brown and the belly is slightly lighter. There is a tuft of darker hair between the horns, while the throat and insides of the ears are white. The ears are short and rounded with a black ridge. The tail becomes darker towards the tip, and ends in white. Both sexes have horns which are short and lie slightly backwards in the line of the face.

Sexual dimorphism: None.

Habitat: Moist riverine bush, mountain bush, thickets in rocky areas and coastal forest, near water.

Habits: Red Duiker are solitary animals, sometimes found in temporary pairs or small groups. They are shy, mainly nocturnal and are seldom seen except on cooler days. They are fond of grazing under trees where monkeys drop wild fruit. When they are alarmed they immediately take cover in thick bush. Red Duiker use communal manure heaps.

Voice: A loud "che-che" whistle when they run away and a whistle-like scream.

Food: Leaves, wild fruit and young shoots.

Gestation period: Unknown.

Breeding: Throughout the year.

Number of young: One.

Mass: 11 – 14 kg (24 – 30 lb).

Shoulder height: ± 43 cm (± 17″).

Life expectancy: ± 12 years.

Record horns: 10,48 cm (4⅛″).

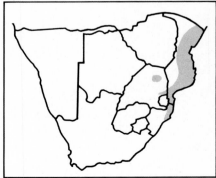

▲ 101 ♂

102 ♀ ▼

51 **COMMON DUIKER** *Sylvicapra grimmia*
(Duiker)

Also known as: Grey Duiker.

Description: The colour of this small antelope varies from yellowish-grey-brown to reddish-yellow-brown with fine speckles. The belly and the inner sides of the limbs are white. The male has a tuft of long black hair between the horns. An outstanding characteristic is the black stripe from the forehead to the nose. There are dark stripes on the front of the fore legs. The tail is narrow, short and white underneath. It differs from the Grysbok by its larger size and by the absence of the white speckles.

Sexual dimorphism: Females are slightly larger than males and lack horns.

Habitat: Areas with enough bush and undergrowth for shade and shelter.

Habits: Common Duiker are usually solitary but form pairs during mating season. They graze or browse early in the morning, late in the afternoon and sometimes at night. They rest during the hottest part of the day in thick shelter. They lie quietly and wait until danger is almost upon them before jumping up. When they run away they dip their heads down and run with characteristic jumping, turning and swinging movements.

Voice: Snorting and a nasal alarm call.

Food: Mainly leaves, but also shoots, flowers, fruit and seeds.

Gestation period: ± 3 months.

Breeding: Throughout the year.

Number of young: One, seldom two.

Mass: ♂ 15 – 21 kg (33 – 46 lb).
♀ 17 – 25 kg (37 – 55 lb).

Shoulder height: ♂ ± 50 cm (± 19″).
♀ ± 52 cm (± 20″).

Life expectancy: ± 10 years.

Record horns: 18,1 cm (7⅛″).

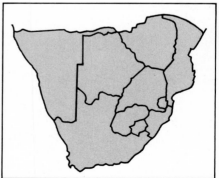

▲ 103 ♂

104 ♀ ▼

52 SPRINGBOK *Antidorcas marsupialis*
(Springbok)

Description: This is South Africa's national animal. The colour is a very light-brown with darker brown stripes along the flanks which separate the light-brown of the body from the white of the belly. On the back is a ridge of long white hair with stripes of brown hair on either side, which is erected when the animal is frightened or when it runs with a characteristic bouncing motion. The face is white with brown stripes from the eyes to the corners of the mouth. Chocolate-brown or predominantly white animals are sometimes found in the same herd with other animals.

Sexual dimorphism: Females are slighter in build than males.

Habitat: Open plains in arid to semi-desert areas.

Habits: Springbok are gregarious animals which form small herds and during the spring congregate into huge herds. Breeding herds, bachelor herds and solitary territorial males also occur. They graze early in the morning and late in the afternoon but rest during the hottest part of the day. Seeing them run is a remarkable experience: The head is kept low down and the hair on the back is upright. They hop with their legs rigid and in this way they are able to jump high and move rapidly over the veld.

Voice: A low pitched growl-bellow, or a high whistling snort alarm call.

Food: Grass, leaves, shoots of karoo bush and herbs.

Gestation period: ± 6 months.

Breeding: Throughout the year with a peak during the summer in summer rainfall areas, and vice versa in winter rainfall areas.

Number of young: One.

Mass: ♂ 33 – 48 kg (73 – 106 lb).
♀ 30 – 44 kg (66 – 97 lb).

Shoulder height: ± 77 cm (± 30").

Life expectancy: ± 10 years.

Record horns: 49,22 cm (19⅜").

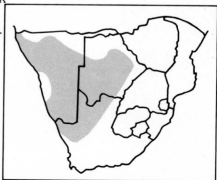

▲ 105 ♂   106 ♀ ▼

53 **KLIPSPRINGER** *Oreotragus oreotragus*
(Klipspringer)

Description: The Klipspringer is a small antelope with a thick spiny coat providing protection against injury when it bumps against the rocks. The colouring varies from yellow to grey-brown to dull grey with fine black speckles providing good camouflage among the rocks. The belly is white and the short tail is the same colour as the body. In front of the eyes are large black tear-shaped markings. The horns are short, upright and bent slightly forward at the tips.

Sexual dimorphism: Females lack horns and are larger than the males.

Habitat: They occur always on or near rocky hills, kopjes or mountains.

Habits: Klipspringer are solitary, found in pairs or family groups. They often stand on high rocks like statues. They can move nimbly, jumping and moving very quickly up steep rock faces, made possible because they move on the tips of their hooves. They rest in the shade during the hottest part of the day and graze early in the morning or late in the afternoon.

Voice: A very loud high forced exhaling of air as alarm call.

Food: Mainly leaves, but sometimes grass.

Gestation period: 7 – 7½ months.

Breeding: Throughout the year.

Number of young: One.

Mass: ♂ 9 – 12 kg (20 – 26 lb).
♀ 11 – 16 kg (24 – 35 lb).

Shoulder height: ± 58 cm (± 23″).

Life expectancy: ± 7 years.

Record horns: 15,9 cm (6¼″).

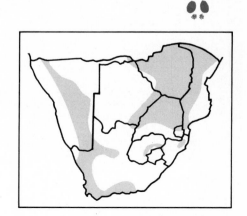

▲ 107 ♂   108 ♀ ▼

54 DAMARA DIK-DIK *Madoqua kirkii*
(Damara dik-dik)

Description: The colour is usually finely speckled grey-brown on the back and buttocks, while the neck, shoulders and flanks are a lighter brown. The areas of the chest, belly and around the eyes are almost white. The horns rise just behind the eyes and slope backwards in the line of the face. Between the horns and on the forehead is a distinguishing tuft of long hair which can be erected. The upper lips are longer than the lower lips.

Sexual dimorphism: Only the males are horned.

Habitat: Prefer dense woodland with shrubs and little grass.

Habits: Damara Dik-dik occur singly or two or three together. Small groups of up to 6 are also seen in dry months. They browse very early in the morning and late in the afternoon, sometimes until after dusk. During the hottest part of the day they rest in dense shade. They always use communal manure heaps. Sometimes when they are frightened, they run with stiff legs bouncing away and giving a loud whistle each time their feet touch the ground.

Voice: A high quivering whistle and a short explosive whistle when disturbed.

Food: Mainly leaves, but also fresh grass shoots. They are not dependent on water.

Gestation period: 5½ – 6 months.

Breeding: December – April.

Number of young: One.

Mass: 4,3 – 5,5 kg (9 – 12 lb).

Shoulder height: ± 39 cm (± 15″).

Life expectancy: ± 9 years.

Record horns: 10,16 cm (4″).

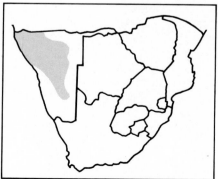

▲ 109 ♂   110 ♀ ▼

55 **Oribi** *Ourebia ourebi*
(Oorbietjie)

Description: A small antelope with light rusty-brown colouring, white throat and belly. The horns are straight but bend slightly forward towards the tips. Next to the nostrils and above the eyes there are white spots. The tail is black on top and white underneath and black spots are present below the ears. It is distinguished from the Steenbok by the black on top of the tail and by being larger, the white area on the belly is bigger and the neck is thinner and longer. It also differs from the Grey Rhebok which is more grey-brown in colour and bigger.

Sexual dimorphism: Females lack horns and are usually slightly larger than males.

Habitat: Open grass plains with or without trees.

Habits: Oribi are solitary animals but sometimes form family herds or temporary herds of up to 12 animals. During the hottest part of the day they rest in the grass. They prefer to graze when it is cooler. When alarmed they leap up and run away in a bouncing fashion. They are inquisitive and after a certain distance will turn around and look back and may even walk back. They use communal manure heaps.

Voice: A snorting alarm whistle.

Food: Grass.

Gestation period: ± 7 months.

Breeding: October – December.

Number of young: One.

Mass: ♂ 11 – 17 kg (24 – 37 lb).
♀ 8 – 20 kg (17 – 44 lb).

Shoulder height: ♂ ± 58 cm (± 22").
♀ ± 59 cm (± 23").

Life expectancy: ± 13 years.

Record horns: 19,05 cm (7½").

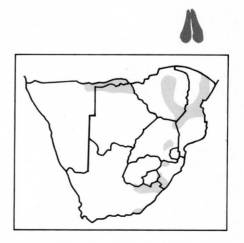

▲111♂   112♀▼

56 STEENBOK *Raphicerus campestris*
(Steenbok)

Description: The colour varies from light brown to a darker brick-brown. The belly, the inside of the legs and underside of the tail are white. The horns are upright, straight and very sharp. It is a small antelope which is still reasonably plentiful. It can be distinguished from the Oribi by the lack of both the black on top of the tail and the black spot underneath the ears. It is also smaller and has a shorter neck than the Oribi.

Sexual dimorphism: Males have horns and are slighter in build than the females.

Habitat: Open areas, avoiding craggy or mountainous terrain.

Habits: Steenbok are solitary animals pairing only during the mating season. During the hottest part of the day they lie down in shade. They graze when it is cooler, even at night. They sometimes share their territory with other Steenbok. They are not very dependent on water. When threatened they often lie flat on the ground but jump up at the last moment, depending on their quick-footed ability to escape.

Voice: A soft bleat.

Food: Grass and leaves but sometimes also roots and bulbs.

Gestation period: ± 6 months.

Breeding: Throughout the year with indications of a peak in November to December.

Number of young: 1, occasionally 2.

Mass: ♂ 9 – 13 kg (20 – 29 lb).
♀ 11 – 13 kg (24 – 29 lb).

Shoulder height: ± 52 cm (± 20″).

Life expectancy: ± 6 years.

Record horns: 19,05 cm (7½″).

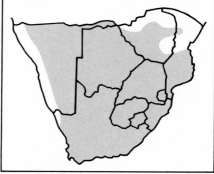

▲ 113 ♂

114 ♀ ▼

57 CAPE GRYSBOK *Raphicerus melanotis*
(Kaapse grysbok)

Description: The colour is dark reddish-brown with white speckles. The colour of the throat, belly and inside of the legs is lighter yellow-brown. It has long pointed ears with short upright horns. It is a small antelope but is slightly smaller and darker in colour than the Sharpe's Grysbok. It differs from the Steenbok by having white speckles on the body and in preferring a more dense habitat.

Sexual dimorphism: Only the males have horns.

Habitat: They prefer bushy undergrowth along rivers and at the foothills of mountains.

Habits: Cape Grysbok are solitary animals, except during the mating season when they are found in pairs. They usually move slowly and carefully with their heads held low. They lie flat on the ground if danger threatens waiting until the last moment before running away. They are mainly nocturnal but also graze in the late afternoon. During the hottest part of the day they rest under thick shelter.

Voice: Bleating screams when caught, otherwise mute.

Food: Mainly grass and leaves but also fruit. They can go without water for long periods.

Gestation period: ± 6 months.

Breeding: September – October.

Number of young: One.

Mass: 9 – 12 kg (20 – 26 lb).

Shoulder height: ± 54 cm (± 21″).

Life expectancy: Unknown.

Record horns: 12,38 cm (± 4⅞″).

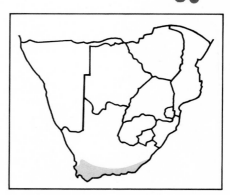

▲ 115 ♂   116 ♀ ▼

58 SHARPE'S GRYSBOK
Raphicerus sharpei
(Tropiese grysbok)

Description: The colour is light brown around the neck and reddish-brown with white speckles on the body. The belly and insides of the legs are white, the horns are very short and upright, the large ears having rounded tips. It is a small antelope differing from the Cape Grysbok by being lighter in colour, having more rounded ears and a more pointed face. It differs from the Steenbok in having white speckles and preferring a denser habitat.

Sexual dimorphism: Females are slightly larger than males and lack horns.

Habitat: Areas with low to medium grass and scrub in woodland.

Habits: Sharpe's Grysbok are solitary animals except during the mating season when they may be seen in pairs. They are mainly nocturnal but also browse during cool cloudy mornings or late afternoons. During the heat of the day they rest under thick shelter. When they are frightened they run away with their heads held low, almost in a crouching position – this distinguishes them from other small antelope.

Voice: Bleating screams when caught, otherwise mute.

Food: Leaves, shoots, roots, fruit and young grass sprouts.

Gestation period: ± 7 months.

Breeding: Throughout the year.

Number of young: One.

Mass: 6,4 – 11,3 kg (14 – 25 lb).

Shoulder height: ±45–50 cm (±17″–19″).

Life expectancy: Unknown.

Record horns: 10,48 cm (4⅛″).

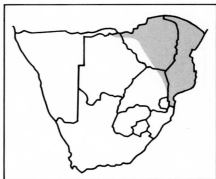

▲ 117 ♂

118 ♀ ▼

59 SUNI *Neotragus moschatus*
(Soenie)

Also known as: Livingstone's Antelope.

Description: This is a very small antelope. The colour varies from dull light-brown to light reddish-brown with lighter speckles on the upper parts. The belly, inside of the legs and throat are white. The tail is long and dark with a white edge and white underneath. The upper lip is longer than the lower and the horns are straight and slope backwards in the line of the face. It can be distinguished from the Steenbok and Duiker by its smaller build, smaller ears, the backward sloping horns and the tail being long and dark with white underneath.

Sexual dimorphism: Only the males have horns and are lighter in build than females.

Habitat: Thickets in dry woodland.

Habits: Suni are very shy and are seldom seen. They are usually solitary but are also found in pairs or family groups. During the hottest part of the day they rest in thick shelter and browse in the early morning and late afternoon. When they are frightened they usually stand dead still for quite some time before running away. They move silently and the continous swinging of their tails is often the only thing which betrays their presence. They use communal manure heaps.

Voice: Snorting and a high "chee-chee" whistle as they run away.

Food: Leaves and fruit. They are not dependent on water.

Gestation period: ± 4 months.

Breeding: August – February.

Number of young: One.

Mass: ♂ 4,5 – 5,2 kg (10 – 12 lb).
♀ 5,1 – 6,8 kg (11 – 15 lb).

Shoulder height: ± 35 cm (± 14").

Life expectancy: Unknown.

Record horns: 13,34 cm (5¼").

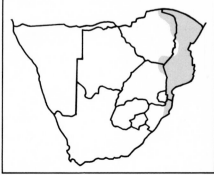

▲ 119 ♂

120 ♀ ▼

60 IMPALA *Aepyceros melampus melampus*
(Rooibok)

Description: The colour of the neck, the buttocks and back is a shining reddish-brown. Halfway down the sides the colour grades to light-brown and then to grey-white on the belly and chest. The eyes are ringed with white hair and there is a dark spot high on the forehead. The three black stripes, as seen from behind on the buttocks and the tail, are characteristic of this species. It has scent-glands on the ankles of the hind legs hidden under a tuft of black hair by which the lamb recognises its mother.

Sexual dimorphism: Females lack horns and are smaller than males.

Habitat: Most types of savannah, but usually avoiding mountainous areas.

Habits: Impala are diurnal living in herds of ± 20 animals. In the winter the herds join to form larger herds. During the mating season the males establish a territory and gather for themselves a group of 15 – 20 females, chasing other males out of their territory with a roaring snort. Non-territorial males and juvenile males form bachelor herds. Impala are very fast and can jump 3 metres high and 12 metres far. Impala still occur outside conservation areas.

Voice: A warning or alarm sneeze, and in the mating season males make a repeated roaring-snort noise.

Food: Leaves and grass.

Gestation period: ± 6½ months.

Breeding: September – January.

Number of young: One.

Mass: ♂ 47 – 82 kg (103 – 180 lb).
♀ 32 – 52 kg (70 – 115 lb).

Shoulder height: ♂ ± 90 cm (± 35″).
♀ ± 86 cm (± 33″).

Life expectancy: ± 12 years.

Record horns: 80,97 cm (31⅞″).

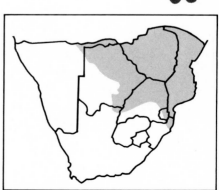

▲ 121 ♂

122 ♀ ▼

61 BLACK-FACED IMPALA
Aepyceros melampus petersi
(Swartneusrooibok)

Description: The colour on the back is dull-brown with a blackish-purple sheen. Along the flanks, between the white belly and the dull-brown on the back, is a strip of light-brown hair. On the face is a black blaze and on the tail and against the back of the buttocks there are vertical black stripes. The cheeks and ears are reddish-brown. They differ from Impala in the black blaze on their faces, longer shaggier tails and the colour of the upper parts being darker and lacking the red sheen of the Impala's coat.

Sexual dimorphism: Only males have horns and they are larger than the females.

Habitat: They prefer dense riverine under growth surrounded by open woodland.

Habits: Black-faced Impala are diurnal animals which form small herds of 3–20, consisting of a male with his females and young ones, while the other males remain solitary. During the lambing season big gatherings take place, which break up later into smaller herds. During the night herds sleep together in open areas. They feed during the cooler part of the day and rest in thickets during the hottest part of the day.

Voice: An alarm sneeze which is sometimes repeated.

Food: Leaves, grass, shoots, flowers and pods.

Gestation period: ± 6½ months.

Breeding: December – January.

Number of young: One.

Mass: ♂ ± 63 kg (± 140 lb).
♀ ± 50 kg (± 110 lb).

Shoulder height: ± 88 cm (± 35″).

Life expectancy: ± 12 years.

Record horns: 67,31 cm (26½″).

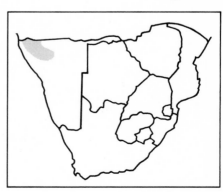

▲ 123 ♂

124 ♀ ▼

62 **GREY RHEBOK** *Pelea capreolus*
(Vaalribbok)

Description: The Grey Rhebok is of medium build and grey-brown in colour, the hair is thick and woolly. The belly and the under parts of the tail are white. The neck is long and thin and the ears are long, upright and pointed which distinguishes it from the Mountain Reedbuck. The horns are straight and upright and conform with the long upright ears. The black spots below the ears, characteristic of the Mountain Reedbuck, are missing, and the horns of the Mountain Reedbuck bend slightly forward.

Sexual dimorphism: Females lack horns and are lighter in build than males.

Habitat: Open mountain slopes or plateaux with grass plains.

Habits: Grey Rhebok are gregarious and form family groups of up to 12 animals which consist of a male, females and young animals. Other males are territorial and solitary. They graze any time of the day with short rest periods but always rest during the hottest part of the day. They are always alert and run away if any danger appears. They run with a rocking motion, the white underparts of the tail showing.

Voice: Snort and an alarm cough.

Food: Exclusively grass.

Gestation period: ± 8½ months.

Breeding: December – January.

Number of young: One.

Mass: 18 – 23 kg (40 – 50 lb).

Shoulder height: ± 74 cm (± 29").

Life expectancy: ± 9 years.

Record horns: 29,21 cm (11½).

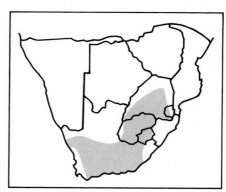

63 ROAN ANTELOPE *Hippotragus equinus*
(Bastergemsbok)

Also known as: Roan.

Description: The Roan Antelope is pale reddish-brown in colour and has a darker upright mane. The legs are slightly darker in colour than the upper parts and the belly is lighter; the tail being dark brown to black. The face is black and mask-like, causing the white patches, in front of the eyes and around the mouth, to be very pronounced. Roans have conspicuously long ears. Both males and females have horns, curving backwards like those of the Sable Antelope, but shorter in length.

Sexual dimorphism: Females are slightly smaller than males and the horns are thinner.

Habitat: Open woodland near water.

Habits: Roan are diurnal animals forming herds of 5 to 25 animals with a dominant female as leader as well as a dominant male. The dominant male defends his females from other males. Young males form small groups, while other adult males are solitary. They graze in the early morning and late afternoon, resting during the heat of the day. Males are often involved in fights, while both sexes defend themselves ably against predators.

Voice: A blowing snort.

Food: Mainly grass, but also leaves and fruit.

Gestation period: 9 – 9½ months.

Breeding: Throughout the year.

Number of young: One.

Mass: 230 – 272 kg (500 – 600 lb).

Shoulder height: ± 143 cm (± 56′).

Life expectancy: ± 19 years.

Record horns: 99,1 cm (39″).

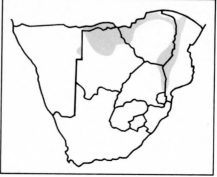

▲ 127 ♂

128 ♀ ▼

64 SABLE ANTELOPE *Hippotragus niger*
(Swartwitpens)

Also known as: Sable.

Description: Both males and females have scimitar-like horns which curve backwards. The colouring is dark brown but this becomes darker with age. The belly and the backside of the buttocks below the tail are white. The female is dark brown in colour whilst the calf is light brown. The face is white with three black stripes, one of which originates between the eyes and goes down to the nose; the other two begin around the eyes and run down the sides of the face to the mouth. The calf looks very similar to the Roan Antelope's calf but it remains close to the parents and can, therefore, not be mistaken.

Sexual dimorphism: Females are slightly smaller, and usually more brown in colour than males and their horns are shorter.

Habitat: Open woodland with medium to long grass.

Habits: These diurnal animals live in herds of between 10 and 40 animals. The herds usually consist of a dominant male, some females with their calves and young animals. Other males remain solitary or form small herds. They normally graze in the early morning or late afternoon and rest during the hottest part of the day. They are able to defend themselves well against all attacks, even those by Lions, by backing up against a bush and awaiting their attackers with head lowered, using their powerful horns with effect.

Voice: Snorting and sneezing.

Food: Mainly grass, but they browse occasionally.

Gestation period: ± 8 months.

Breeding: January – March.

Number of young: One.

Mass: 180 –250 kg (400 – 550 lb).

Shoulder height: ± 140 cm (± 55″).

Life expectancy: ± 17 years.

Record horns: 154,3 cm (60¾″).

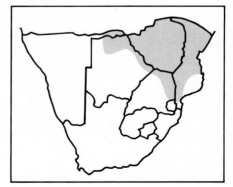

▲ 129 ♂   130 ♀ ▼

65 GEMSBOK *Oryx gazella*
(Gemsbok)

Description: The colour varies from light brown to ash grey with lighter patches on the buttocks. The tail is black with long hair. It has a dark brown stripe low down on the flanks which joins up with the dark brown on the upper legs. The rest of the legs and the belly are white. On the croup is a patch of brown which joins up with the brown on the top of the back. The face is white with a black patch on the snout. A smaller black patch high on the forehead, and two black stripes beginning around the eyes, go down the sides of the face and join the black stripe on the throat. Both sexes have the characteristic long straight horns.

Sexual dimorphism: Females are lighter in build than males and the horns are longer and thinner.

Habitat: Plains in dry open savannah and semi-desert regions.

Habits: Gemsbok live in herds of 12 or more animals. Adult males are territorial and are solitary or form small herds of 2-3. Other herds consist of females, juveniles and calves. After birth, calves are hidden for a few months before they are brought into the herd by their mothers. Gemsbok often kneel while grazing and can survive for long periods without water.

Voice: Bellow like cattle.

Food: Mainly grass. They will also dig for succulent tubers and eat tsamma melons and other fruit.

Gestation period: ± 9 months.

Breeding: Throughout the year.

Number of young: One.

Mass: ♂ ± 240 kg (± 530 lb).
♀ ± 210 kg (± 460 lb).

Shoulder height: ± 120 cm (± 47″).

Life expectancy: ± 19 years.

Record horns: 122,9 cm (48⅜″).

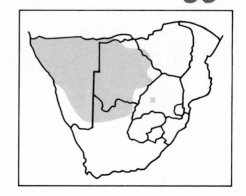

▲ 131 ♂   132 ♀ ▼

66 BUFFALO *Syncerus caffer*
(Buffel)

Description: The colour of the juvenile is light reddish-brown, the male darkening with age until it is a grey-black colour. The mature male is darker than the female which retains a reddish-brown tinge. The animal is fond of wallowing in mud and consequently takes on the colour of the soil. Both sexes are horned, and the horns of the male are especially large with broad thick bosses. The ears are situated below the horns.

Sexual dimorphism: Males are more heavily built and have bigger and heavier horns than females.

Habitat: Any type of savannah usually near water.

Habits: Buffalo are diurnal animals living in herds of up to many hundreds. Old males are solitary or form small herds. They usually graze at night or during the cooler parts of the day and like to sleep on bare spots of ground. They are inquisitive animals with an acute sense of smell but with poor eyesight and hearing. They are known as being one of the most dangerous animals to hunt because, when wounded, they circle back and wait for a chance to attack the hunter.

Voice: Bellow like cattle.

Food: Mainly grass, but sometimes shoots and leaves as well.

Gestation period: ± 11 months.

Breeding: August – February.

Number of young: One.

Mass: ♂ 750 – 820 kg (1 650 – 1 800 lb).
♀ 680 – 750 kg (1 500 – 1 650 lb).

Shoulder height: ±140 – 170 cm (55″ – 67″)

Life expectancy: ± 23 years.

Record horns: 127,3 cm (50⅛″).

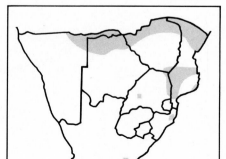

▲ 133 ♂

134 ♀ ▼

67 KUDU *Tragelaphus strepsiceros*
(Koedoe)

Description: The Kudu is a big antelope with a stately bearing. The colour is pale-grey to brownish-grey with a number of vertical white stripes on the flanks. The male becomes darker on the neck as it ages. Between the eyes there is a white "v" chevron marking. Females look similar to the males but without the horns their ears are very prominent, being large and rounded, with a white fringe. The tail is white underneath and there is a conspicuous hump on the shoulders.

Sexual dimorphism: Females are smaller than males and lack the horns.

Habitat: Savannah with enough trees or scrub.

Habits: Kudu are diurnal animals which browse in the early morning and in the late afternoon. They form family groups of 5–12 animals, consisting mostly of females and calves, except in the mating season. Males form separate herds or become solitary. They are graceful and athletic and can jump very high for such large animals (± 2 metres). If the males move fast through trees they keep their heads tilted backwards with their horns on their backs. Kudu are still fairly common outside conservation areas.

Voice: A very loud bark.

Food: Leaves, growing points of plants, pods and sometimes fresh grass.

Gestation period: ± 7 months.

Breeding: November – January.

Number of young: One.

Mass: ♂ 190 – 270 kg (420 – 600 lb).
♀ 120 – 210 kg (264 – 460 lb).

Shoulder height: ♂ ± 150 cm (± 59″).
♀ ± 135 cm (± 53″).

Life expectancy: ± 14 years.

Record horns: 170,18 cm (67″).

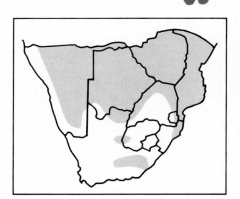

▲ 135 ♂   136 ♀ ▼

68 SITATUNGA *Tragelaphus spekei*
(Waterkoedoe)

Description: A shy antelope with long hair and a white chevron mark between the eyes. The colour of the male is dark grey-brown while the female is usually lighter, yellowish- to reddish-brown with distinct white spots on the flanks and buttocks. The vertical white stripes on the flanks are usually absent or very faint in Southern Africa. There is a white patch on the throat and a white band at the base of the neck. The hooves are very long and splayed to assure a good, firm tread on wet muddy ground. They are larger than Bushbucks and have longer horns.

Sexual dimorphism: Females are much smaller, lack horns and are usually lighter in colour than males.

Habitat: Confined to the permanent swamps of Botswana and the Eastern Caprivi.

Habits: Sitatungu are usually solitary or in pairs, but are always connected to a small loosely knit herd of up to 6 animals consisting of a male, a few females and juveniles. They can swim well and if disturbed take to the water. During the day they feed in the reed and papyrus beds in the swamps avoiding open floodplains. They rest during the heat of the day on platforms formed from dry reeds and other vegetation. During the night they sometimes move to surrounding dry woodland and return to the swamps again before daylight.

Voice: A repeated alarm bark.

Food: The umbels of papyrus, young reeds and aquatic grasses.

Gestation period: Unknown.

Breeding: Throughout the year with a peak in June – July.

Number of young: One.

Mass: ♂ ± 114 kg (± 250 lb).
♀ ± 55 kg (± 120 lb).

Shoulder height: ♂ ± 114 cm (± 45").
♀ ± 90 cm (± 35").

Life expectancy: ± 19 years.

Record horns: 92,4 cm (36⅜").

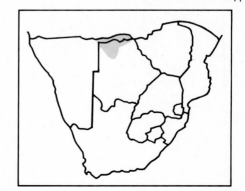

▲ 137 ♂   138 ♀ ▼

69 NYALA *Tragelaphus angasii*
(Njala)

Description: The Nyala is slenderly built with a thin body and moves gracefully. The male is dark blue-grey in colour with white vertical stripes, yellow stockinged legs and a white chevron mark between the eyes. The mane on the neck and back is white tipped. Old males have a long fringe of hair under the belly and against the backside of the buttocks. The female is reddish-brown to chestnut with the same stripes and marks but lacks the chevron between the eyes. The female differs from the Bushbuck female by having more vertical stripes and being larger.

Sexual dimorphism: Only the males have horns. They are darker in colour and larger than females.

Habitat: Thickets and dense bush along rivers in dry woodland.

Habits: Nyala live in small, loosely knit herds of 3–16 animals. The herd consists of one male, females and young. Members move freely between groups. Old males are solitary or form small herds. They browse by day and night, especially late afternoon and rest during the hottest part of the day. They are fond of browsing under trees where baboons and monkeys have dislodged fruit.

Voice: A bleat and a deep bellow-bark.

Food: Mainly leaves but also freshly sprouting grasses, fruit, flowers and pods.

Gestation period: ± 7 months.

Breeding: Throughout the year with a main peak from August to December and a secondary peak in May.

Number of young: One.

Mass: ♂ 92 – 126 kg (200 – 280 lb).
♀ 55 – 68 kg (120 – 150 lb).

Shoulder height: ♂ ± 112 cm (± 44″).
♀ ± 97 cm (± 38″).

Life expectancy: ± 13 years.

Record horns: 82,55 cm (32½″).

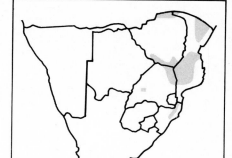

▲ 139 ♂

140 ♀ ▼

70 **BUSHBUCK** *Tragelaphus scriptus*
(Bosbok)

Description: The colouring of the male varies from brown to dark brown and that of the female from light brown to chestnut. Both sexes have white spots on the legs, a white patch on the throat and a white band at the base of the neck. There are white spots on the buttocks and the tip of the tail is also white. Some animals have vertical white stripes, which are characteristic of the reddish-brown coloured Chobe Bushbuck, which has more white spots on the flanks. The female differs from the nyala female by being smaller and having fewer or even no vertical stripes.

Sexual dimorphism: Females are smaller, lack horns and are lighter in colour than males.

Habitat: Thickets or riverine bush near water.

Habits: Bushbuck are shy solitary antelope but pairs or small groups of females and young animals are found. The males are very couragous and will attack and sometimes kill Leopards, dogs and even human beings. They rest during the day in thickets coming out late in the afternoon and grazing until late at night. All their senses are well developed which is probably why they still survive outside conservation areas.

Voice: A loud bark like that of a Baboon.

Food: Mainly leaves, and sometimes grass.

Gestation period: ± 6 months.

Breeding: Throughout the year.

Number of young: One.

Mass: ♂ 40 – 77 kg (88 – 170 lb).
♀ 30 – 36 kg (66 – 80 lb).

Shoulder height: ♂ ± 80 cm (± 32").
♀ ± 70 cm (± 28").

Life expectancy: ± 11 years.

Record horns: 55,25 cm (21¾").

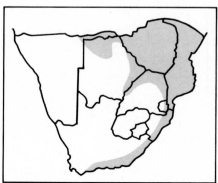

▲ 141 ♂

142 ♀ ▼

71 **ELAND** *Taurotragus oryx*
(Eland)

Description: The Eland is the region's largest antelope. The colour is greyish-brown, the male developing a blueish-grey neck as it grows older. Faint vertical white stripes are sometimes seen down the flanks. A grown male reminds one of a Brahman bull because of the hump and the dewlap. Both sexes have straight horns with a slightly curved edge, a tassel of long brown hair on the forehead and dark brown hair along the top of the back.

Sexual dimorphism: Males are larger than females, with shorter and stouter horns.

Habitat: Widely spread, but they prefer open woodland and shrubby flat veld.

Habits: Eland usually form small herds, from 8–12 animals, but very large herds are not uncommon. They usually graze during the day, but in the rainy season they will sometimes graze well into the night, ranging widely in search of food. Eland are nervous animals, taking flight at the least sign of danger. They are surprisingly good jumpers, considering their bulk, clearing a height of 2 metres with ease. Serious fights between males sometimes occur.

Voice: Females "moo", calves bleat and males bellow – also sometimes make a barking sound.

Food: Leaves, and grass in the spring.

Gestation period: ± 9 months.

Breeding: Throughout the year with a peak in August – October.

Number of young: One.

Mass: ♂ ± 700 kg (± 1 540 lb).
♀ ± 460 kg (± 1 012 lb).

Shoulder height: ♂ ± 170 cm (± 67").
♀ ± 150 cm (± 59").

Life expectancy: ± 12 years.

Record horns: 102,2 cm (40¼").

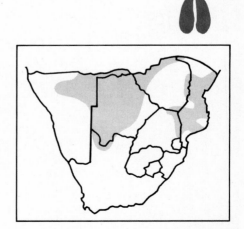

143

▲ 143 ♂

144 ♀ ▼

72 REEDBUCK *Redunca arundinum*
(Rietbok)

As known as: Southern Reedbuck.

Description: The colour of the body is a yellowish grey-brown, the throat and chest grey-white and the belly white. The fronts of the fore legs are dark brown and there are often small black glandular areas below the ears. The tail is bushy, with white underneath. It could be confused with the Impala and the Mountain Reedbuck: the three black stripes seen on the hindquarters of the Impala are missing and the Impala is redder than the Reedbuck. The Mountain Reedbuck is smaller and more greyish and the habitat differs.

Sexual dimorphism: Only the males have horns, and they are larger than females.

Habitat: Vleis, reedbeds and dry floodplains.

Habits: They usually appear in pairs or family groups, while larger groups are also seen temporarily during the winter months. They are always near water. During the heat of day they rest in reedbeds or long grass, grazing during the cooler parts of the day and even during the night. They run with a typical rocking horse movement with the tail held high showing the white underneath.

Voice: A high alarm whistle.

Food: Grass.

Gestation period: 7½ – 8 months.

Breeding: Throughout the year.

Number of young: One.

Mass: ♂ ± 80 kg (± 175 lb).
♀ ± 70 kg (± 155 lb).

Shoulder height: ♂ ± 90 cm (± 35″).
♀ ± 80 cm (± 32″).

Life expectancy: ± 9 years.

Record horns: 45,7 cm (18″).

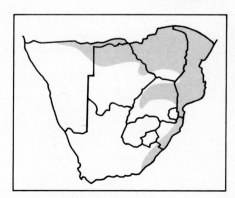

▲ 145 ♂   146 ♀ ▼

73 MOUNTAIN REEDBUCK
Redunca fulvorufula
(Rooiribbok)

Description: A medium sized antelope with a long haired coat. The colour varies from grey to reddish-brown and the neck is always brown. The belly is white, the tail bushy with white underneath and there are black spots below the ears. It differs from the Grey Rhebok which is more grey-brown, has a longer neck and more pointed and upright ears. The horns of the Mountain Reedbuck bend forward about the level of the tips of the ears which are rounded with a white fringe.

Sexual dimorphism: The males are slightly larger than females, which are hornless.

Habitat: Rocky slopes of mountains, hills and kopjes.

Habits: Mountain Reedbuck are gregarious, living in herds of 3–6 animals, but bigger herds have also been observed. Males are solitary or form bachelor herds, while other herds consist of females and juveniles. They are wary and inquisitive. During the heat of day they usually rest in the shade. They graze and drink water early in the morning, the late afternoon or even at night. They run with a typical rocking horse movement, the white underparts of the tail showing.

Voice: A sharp alarm whistle.

Food: Mainly grass.

Gestation period: ± 8 months.

Breeding: Throughout the year with a peak in December – January.

Number of young: One.

Mass: ♂ 24 – 36 kg (53 – 80 lb).
♀ 15 – 34 kg (33 – 75 lb).

Shoulder height: ± 73 cm (± 29″).

Life expectancy: ± 11 years.

Record horns: 34,29 cm (13½″).

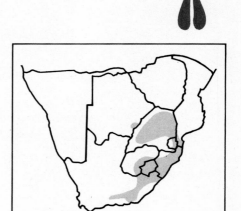

▲ 147 ♂

148 ♀ ▼

74 WATERBUCK *Kobus ellipsiprymnus*
(Waterbok)

Description: The Waterbuck is a big antelope with a characteristic white circle around the tail and a collar of white hair around the neck. The colour of the rest of the body is grey-brown. There are white stripes on the ridges of the eyebrows and the chin is white. The tuft on the end of the tail as well as the lower legs are darker and more brown in colour. The hair is shaggy, coarse and long.

Sexual dimorphism: The males are larger than the females, which are hornless.

Habitat: Areas near rivers or marshes, never far from water.

Habits: Waterbuck are diurnal, gregarious animals. The small herds of 6–12 animals consist mostly of females, calves and young. Males are territorial and whilst some remain solitary, others go with the herds. Serious fights between male Waterbuck are more common than similar fights in other species of antelope. If danger threatens they flee into the water, even if there are crocodiles. Crocodiles do not usually attack them, probably on account of an unpleasant smell given off from their skin.

Voice: Not often heard. Snoring sound when alarmed or excited. Female calls calf with a soft "muh".

Food: Grass, sometimes leaves.

Gestation period: ± 9 months.

Breeding: Throughout the year.

Number of young: One, seldom two.

Mass: ♂ 250 – 270 kg (550 – 600 lb).
♀ 205 – 250 kg (450 – 550 lb).

Shoulder height: ♂ ± 170 cm (± 67″).
♀ ± 130 cm (± 51″).

Life expectancy: ± 14 years.

Record horns: 99,7 cm (39¼″).

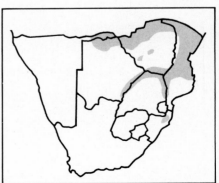

▲ 149 ♂

150 ♀ ▼

75 RED LECHWE *Kobus leche*
(Basterwaterbok)

Description: An usually built medium sized antelope with the shoulders lower than the croup causing the body to slant forward. The colouring is a bright reddish-brown, lighter lower down the body, and becoming white on the belly. The throat is white and there are characteristic black stripes on the front legs. The hooves are somewhat splayed and longer than other antelope, ensuring a better footing in marshy areas.

Sexual dimorphism: The female is smaller than the male and lacks horns.

Habitat: Permanent swamps and floodplains.

Habits: Red Lechwe form herds ranging in numbers from 10–100+ animals, although they are usually found in smaller herds of 10–20. They are good swimmers and are able to run easily through shallow water. If danger threatens they flee into the water. They cannot move fast on dry land and run with their heads held characteristically low. They are seen at any time of the day, when they graze knee-deep in the water, especially early in the morning and late afternoon. During the hottest part of the day they rest on dry islands in the swamp, and at night they sleep near the waterside.

Voice: Whinnying-grunt as a warning call and a low-pitched whistling sound.

Food: Watergrass and other grass on the fringes of swamps.

Gestation period: 7 – 8 months.

Breeding: Throughout the year, with a peak in October – December.

Number of young: One.

Mass: ♂ 100 – 130 kg (220 – 290 lb).
♀ 61 – 97 kg (135 – 215 lb).

Shoulder height: ♂ ± 104 cm (± 41″).
♀ ± 97 cm (± 38″).

Life expectancy: Unknown.

Record horns: 93,98 cm (37″).

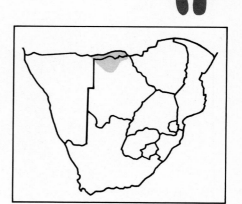

▲ 151 ♂   152 ♀ ▼

76 **PUKU** *Kobus vardonii*
(Poekoe)

Description: The Puku is a well-built medium sized antelope with a horizontal back. The colouring is a yellowish gold-brown over most of the body. Under the belly the colour is slightly lighter, and darker on the forehead. A small area above the eyes and around the mouth is white and there is a black edge to the back of the ears. It can be distinguished from the Lechwe by the smaller size and because it lacks the black stripes on the front legs.

Sexual dimorphism: Females are smaller than males and lack horns.

Habitat: The grassplains between swamps and the surrounding woodlands.

Habits: Puku form herds of 6–20 animals consisting of females and young. Adult males are territorial and are solitary, while other males form bachelor herds. Members move freely between herds. During the mating season the male rounds up a number of females passing through his territory. One of his major occupations is then to keep his females together. They usually graze early in the morning and in the late afternoon, even until after dark.

Voice: A repeated alarm whistle.

Food: Mainly grass, but they sometimes browse on thorn trees.

Gestation period: ± 8 months.

Breeding: Throughout the year, with a peak in May – September.

Number of young: One.

Mass: ♂ 68 – 91 kg (150 – 200 lb).
♀ 48 – 80 kg (105 – 176 lb).

Shoulder height: ♂ ± 81 cm (± 32″).
♀ ± 78 cm (± 30″).

Life expectancy: Unknown.

Record horns: 53,98 cm (21¼″).

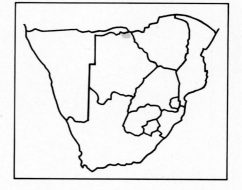

▲ 153

154 ▼

77 PANGOLIN *Manis temminckii*
(Ietermagog)

Description: The very hard dark grey-brown scales which cover the body like roof tiles are an outstanding feature of the species. The sides of the face are devoid of scales. It has a small head and pointed snout. It walks on the hindlegs with the front legs held off the ground, touching it now and then. The fore feet are equipped with long curved claws with which it digs. It is an odd animal and is very seldom seen.

Sexual dimorphism: None.

Habitat: They prefer sandy soil in very dry to fairly humid types of savannah.

Habits: Pangolins are usually solitary and move noisily as they brush against bushes and branches. They are mainly nocturnal but are sometimes seen during the day. If they suspect any intrusion, they stand upright on their hindlegs, supported by their tails. They live in old Antbear holes and hunt for food at night. If they are threatened they roll themselves into a ball. They can give off a bad odour when frightened.

Voice: An audible snuffling when feeding and a hiss when rolling in a ball.

Food: Mainly ants and sometimes termites.

Gestation period: ± 4½ months.

Breeding: May – July.

Number of young: One.

Mass: 4,5 – 14,5 kg (10 – 32 lb).

Length: ± 81 cm (± 32″).

Life expectancy: ± 12 years.

H   F

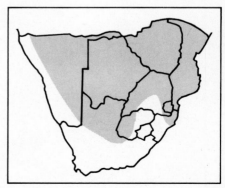

78 CAPE HARE *Lepus capensis*
(Vlakhaas)

Description: The colour varies between two extremes. Some animals are a dull-yellow with black-grey speckles, the patch on the nape of the neck brown-pink and the tail black on top and white underneath. Others are grey-white, the patch on the nape of the neck light grey and the tail dull black and white underneath. Around the eyes the Cape Hare has fringes of light yellow hair, and just above the eyes are oblong light brown spots. It differs from the Scrub Hare in being smaller and preferring more open areas.

Sexual dimorphism: Females are slightly larger than males.

Habitat: Open grassy plains with patches of tall grass for shelter.

Habits: Cape Hares are solitary nocturnal animals which are seen only on cloudy days, or at sunrise and sunset. They are very sensitive to weather conditions. They are not seen often on cold nights and remain in their shelters when it rains. During the day they rest in the shelter of tall grass or small bushes, lying down with their ears flat. In this position they lie dead still until danger is very close, before jumping up. They run remarkably fast turning and swinging easily at high speed. They sometimes take shelter in old Antbear or Springhare holes.

Voice: Quiet animals, but make a soft grunt and scream loudly when handled.

Food: Grazers with a preference for areas of short grass.

Gestation period: ± 5 weeks.

Breeding: Throughout the year, peaking in summer.

Number of young: 1 – 3.

Mass: ♂ 1,4 – 1,8 kg (3 – 4 lb).
♀ 1,5 – 2,3 kg (3,3 – 5 lb).

Length: ± 47 cm (± 18½").

Life expectancy: ± 5 years.

H   F

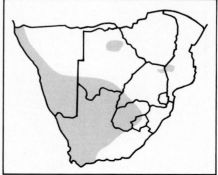

▲ 157

158 ▼

79 SCRUB HARE *Lepus saxatilis*
(Kolhaas)

Description: It is the larger of the two hares. The colour is a dull yellow with black-grey speckles, giving a salt and pepper effect. The chin and stomach are white and the throat is surrounded by a collar which is the same colour as the upper parts. A white spot on the forehead is situated just above the eyes, and a patch on the nape of the neck varies in colour from brick-red to orange-yellow. The tail is black on top and white underneath and the feet are a dull-yellow colour. It is distinguished from the Cape Hare by its larger size and a preference for a more shrubby area.

Sexual dimorphism: Females are slightly larger than males.

Habitat: Areas with enough grass or thicket.

Habits: Scrub Hares are nocturnal, appearing only at sunset; at sunrise they return to their shelters. During cloudy weather they may graze in the mornings. They are sensitive to weather conditions, on cold evenings they are less active, and in rainy weather they remain in their shelters. During the day they rest under bushes with their heads and ears flat down. Usually they are solitary but also appear in pairs. They still occur outside conservation areas.

Voice: Quiet animals, but they may scream loudly if handled.

Food: Leaves, stems, rhizomes of grasses and green grass.

Gestation period: ± 5 weeks.

Breeding: Throughout the year.

Number of young: 1 – 3.

Mass: ♂ 1,4 – 3,8 kg (3 – 8 lb).
♀ 1,6 – 4,5 kg (3,5 – 10 lb).

Length: ± 55 cm (± 22″).

Life expectancy: ± 7½ years.

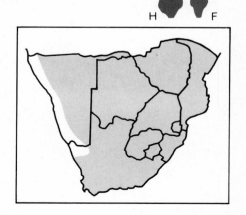

▲ 159

160 ▼

80 GROUND SQUIRREL *Xerus inauris*
(Waaierstert-grondeekhoring)

Description: The colour of the body is a light cinnamon with characteristic white stripes along the flanks. The lower parts of the legs, the belly, along the sides of the neck and around the eyes are white. The hair of the tail is long, it is ringed with black and white, and has a white tip. When it stands on its hindlegs the tail is like an open fan spread to give shade to its back and head. The ears are simple openings in the side of the head. It is very difficult to distinguish between the Ground Squirrel and the Mountain Ground Squirrel in the field. The Mountain Ground Squirrel prefers a habitat on rocky hillsides, which is normally avoided by the Ground Squirrel.

Sexual dimorphism: Males are slightly larger than females.

Habitat: Open plains with hard soil and thinly spread bushes.

Habits: Ground Squirrels are diurnal and live in colonies of up to 30 animals. They dig their own burrows, about 80 cm (2,5') underneath the ground, with many tunnels, corridors and entrances. Rooms in the burrows are lined with grass on which they rest. Such a burrow is occupied by a few females with their young. The dominant female chases away all strangers from the immediate vicinity of the entrance. Males move from one group to another and stay only for a few weeks. They move only after sunrise and return to the burrow before sunset.

Voice: A high whistle or screaming alarm call, and an aggressive growl.

Food: Leaves, grass, stems, bulbs, seeds, roots and sometimes insects.

H   F

Gestation period: 6 – 7 weeks.

Breeding: Throughout the year.

Number of young: 1 – 3.

Mass: ♂ 511 – 1 022 g (1,1 – 2,2 lb).
♀ 511 – 795 g (1,1 – 1,7 lb).

Length: ± 45 cm (± 17,7″).

Life expectancy: ± 15 years.

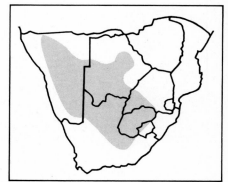

▲ 161

162 ▼

81 **TREE SQUIRREL** *Paraxerus cepapi*
(Boomeekhoring)

Description: The colour is variable: The upper parts of the body vary from a speckled grey with a buffy tinge, to a speckled rusty colour. The flanks are always more yellowish and the under parts vary from white to buff. In the Transvaal the limbs are yellowish without speckles. The tail is long and bushy and is indistinctly ringed with black. It differs from the Red Squirrel whose tail, belly and legs are more yellow or red than the body. The Striped Tree Squirrel is smaller and has white stripes on its flanks, the Sun Squirrel is larger and the tail, as a whole, is ringed with white.

Sexual dimorphism: None.

Habitat: A woodland species, living in mixed thornveld or mopani woodland.

Habits: They forage alone but in the Transvaal they live in groups consisting of one or two males, females and their young. Members of the group get used to each other's smell and strangers are chased away. They feed mostly on the ground and scatter to the nearest tree when they perceive danger. They have an acute sense of hearing and are always watchful.

Voice: A stretched "chook chook chook" sound which gets louder and follows more rapidly till it changes to a rattling sound.

Food: Leaves, flowers, seeds, fruit, bark, berries and sometimes insects.

Gestation period: ± 8 weeks.

Breeding: Throughout the year, with a peak in October – April.

Number of young: 1 – 3.

Mass: ♂ 76 – 240 g (2½ – 8½ oz).
♀ 108 – 265 g (3¾ – 9½ oz).

Length: ± 35 cm (± 14″).

Life expectancy: ± 8 years.

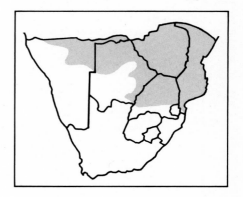

82 **SPRINGHARE** *Pedetes capensis*
(Springhaas)

Description: These rodents resemble Kangaroos, the fore-legs being short, and the hind-legs very long and powerful. The colour varies from a light fawnish-brown to yellow-brown. The chin is white and the lower parts offwhite. The long tail is reddish ending in a broad black tip. The eyes are conspicuously large, and they have long black whiskers. Strong, curved claws on the fore-feet are adapted to digging. The ears are narrow and upright.

Sexual dimorphism: None.

Habitat: Along rivers or pans with sandy soil. They avoid hard ground.

Habits: Springhare are exclusively nocturnal, emerging from their burrows well after dark. The burrows, excavated on high ground to avoid flooding, branch out into passages, some having different entrances. A burrow is occupied by a single animal. They are accomplished diggers, loosening the soil with the fore-paws and pushing it out with their powerful hindlegs. They move with a hopping motion, using the hind-legs only, all the while keeping the short fore-legs held close to the body.

Voice: Silent, but scream loudly when handled.

Food: Grass, leaves, roots, rhizomes and corms.

Gestation period: ± 10½ weeks.

Breeding: Throughout the year.

Number of young: One. Exceptionally 2.

Mass: 2,5 – 3,8 kg (5½ – 8½ *lb*).

Length: ± 80 cm (± 31″).

Life expectancy: ± 7 years.

H   F

▲ 165

166 ▼

83 PORCUPINE *Hystrix africaeaustralis*
(Ystervark)

Description: The largest rodent in the region. The body is covered with quills, spines and flattened black bristles. The quills are white with black rings and are about 30 cm (12″) long. On the neck and back the quills and spines are longer and thinner and can be erected, which makes them look large and fearsome. The rest of the body, the face and the short legs are covered with coarse black hair.

Sexual dimorphism: Females are usually larger than males.

Habitat: They are very adaptable and are found in most types of habitat except in forests and deserts.

Habits: Porcupine are usually solitary, but three or more adults may make use of the same shelter. Sometimes they move long distances at night seeking food. They can run fast if chased. They cause much damage in agricultural lands and vegetable gardens. Quills are not shot off but they back up to the attacker so that the quills stick and remain in the attacker. Sometimes Lions and Leopards have trouble after an attack when quills, which have broken off, cause festering sores.

Voice: Growl, snuffle and rattle their tail quills when frightened.

Food: Bulbs, tubers, roots which they dig out, also vegetables like pumpkins and watermelons.

Gestation period: ± 3 months.

Breeding: Throughout the year.
In summer rain regions: August – March.

Number of young: 1 – 4.

Mass: ♂ 10 – 19 kg (22 – 42 lb).
♀ 10 – 24 kg (22 – 53 lb).

Length: ± 84 cm (± 33″).

Life expectancy: ± 8 years.

H   F

167

BIBLIOGRAPHY

BROWN, L. 1972. *The Life on the African Plains.* New York: McGraw-Hill.

BRYANT, E.R. 1984. *Rowland Ward's African Records of Big Game. xix edition,* San Antonio, Texas: Rowland Ward Publications, a division of Game Conservation International.

CLARKE J. & PITTS, J. 1972. *Focus on Fauna: the Wildlife of South Africa.* Johannesburg: Nelson.

DORST, J. & DANDELOT, P. 1972. *A Field Guide to the Mammals of Africa including Madagascar.* London: Collins.

MABERLEY, C.T.A. 1963. *The Game Animals of Southern Africa.* Johannesburg: Nelson.

MEESTER, J.A.J. & SETZER, H.W. 1971. *The Mammals of Africa: An Identification Manual.* Washington D.C.: Smithsonian Institution.

NATIONAL PARKS BOARD OF SOUTH AFRICA. 1980. *Mammals of the Kruger and other National Parks.* Pretoria: National Parks Board of South Africa.

PIENAAR, U. DE V., RAUTENBACH, I.L. & DE GRAAF, G. 1980. *The Small Mammals of the Kruger National Park.* Pretoria: National Parks Board of South Africa.

PLAYER, I. 1972. *Big Game.* Cape Town: Caltex.

ROBERTS, A. 1952. *The Mammals of South Africa.* Johannesburg: C.N.A.

ROEDELBERGER, F. & GROSCHOFF, V. 1964. *African Wildlife.* London: Constable.

ROSE, P. 1968. *Big Game and Other Mammals.* Cape Town – Johannesburg: Purnell.

SHORTRIDGE, G.C. 1934. *The Mammals of South West Africa.* London: Heinemann.

SKINNER, J. & BANNISTER, A. 1985. *Wild Animals of South Africa.* Johannesburg: C.N.A.

SMITHERS, R.H.N. 1966. *The Mammals of Rhodesia, Zambia and Malawi.* London: Collins.

SMITHERS, R.H.N. 1983. *The Mammals of the Southern Africa Subregion.* Pretoria: University of Pretoria.

STEVENSON HAMILTON, J. *Wildlife in South Africa.* London: Cassel.

YOUNG, E.J., DEEKS, J. & LANDMAN, M. 1978. *Beskerm ons Seldsame Spesies Soogdiere van die Transvaal.* Johannesburg: E. Stanton.

ZALOUMIS, E.A. & CROSS, R. *A Field Guide to the Antelope of Southern Africa.* Durban: Natal Branch of The Wildlife Society of Southern Africa.

PHOTOGRAPHIC ACKNOWLEDGEMENTS

INDEX

GUIDE

FOR THE USE OF THE IDENTI-INDEX AND SPOOR ILLUSTRATIONS

The following pages give an illustrated index of the animals listed in this book, followed by three pages of their spoors (or tracks).

The alternate shading of the Identi-Index and spoor charts group the animals into their types and further assists in rapid identification.

Some examples of the size determination

very small	–	eg: Hedgehog, Squirrel
small	–	eg: Steenbok, Vervet Monkey
medium	–	eg: Warthog, Baboon
large	–	eg: Kudu, Lion
very large	–	eg: Elephant, Giraffe

1 **South African Hedgehog** (very small)			**9** **Black-backed Jackal** (small)
2 **Chacma Baboon** (medium)			**10** **Cape Clawless Otter** (small)
3 **Vervet Monkey** (small)			**11** **Honey Badger** (small)
4 **Samango Monkey** (small)			**12** **Striped Polecat** (very small)
5 **Bat-eared Fox** (small)			**13** **African Civet** (small)
6 **Wild Dog** (medium)			**14** **Large-spotted Genet** (very small)
7 **Cape Fox** (small)			**15** **Suricate** (very small)
8 **Side-striped Jackal** (small)			**16** **Yellow Mongoose** (very small)
			17 **Water Mongoose** (very small)

18 **Banded Mongoose** (very small)		26 **Caracal** (small)
19 **Dwarf Mongoose** (very small)		27 **Serval** (small)
20 **Aardwolf** (medium)		28 **Small Spotted Cat** (very small)
		29 **African Wild Cat** (small)
21 **Brown Hyaena** (medium)		30 **Elephant** (very large)
22 **Spotted Hyaena** (medium)		
23 **Cheetah** (medium)		31 **Cape Mountain Zebra** (large)
24 **Leopard** (medium)		
25 **Lion** (large)		32 **Hartmann's Mountain Zebra** (large)

175

33 **Burchell's Zebra** (large)		

34 **Square-lipped** **Rhinoceros** (very large)		**40** **Hippopotamus** (very large)

35
Hook-lipped
Rhinoceros
(very large)

41
Giraffe
(very large)

36
Rock Dassie
(very small)

37
Antbear
(medium)

42
Black Wildebeest
(large)

38
Warthog
(medium)

43
Blue Wildebeest
(large)

39
Bushpig
(medium)

44
Lichtenstein's
Hartebeest
(large)

45
Red Hartebeest
(large)

46
Bontebok
(medium)

47
Blesbok
(medium)

48
Tsessebe
(large)

49
Blue Duiker
(small)

50
Red Duiker
(small)

51
Common Duiker
(small)

52
Springbok
(medium)

53
Klipspringer
(small)

54
Damara Dik-dik
(small)

55
Oribi
(small)

56
Steenbok
(small)

57
Cape Grysbok
(small)

58
Sharpe's Grysbok
(small)

59
Suni
(small)

60
Impala
(medium)
61
Black-faced
Impala
(medium)

62
Grey Rhebok
(medium)

63
Roan Antelope
(large)

64
Sable Antelope
(large)

65
Gemsbok
(large)

66
Buffalo
(very large)

67
Kudu
(large)

68
Sitatunga
(large)

69
Nyala
(large)

70
Bushbuck
(medium)

71
Eland
(very large)

72
Reedbuck
(medium)

73
Mountain
Reedbuck
(medium)

74
Waterbuck
(large)

75
Red Lechwe
(medium)

76
Puku
(medium)

77
Pangolin
(small)

78
Cape Hare
(small)

79
Scrub Hare
(small)

80
Ground Squirrel
(very small)

81
Tree Squirrel
(very small)

82
Springhare
(small)

83
Porcupine
(small)

SPOORS

Spoor shown is of the hindfoot unless indicated

F = Fore   H = Hind

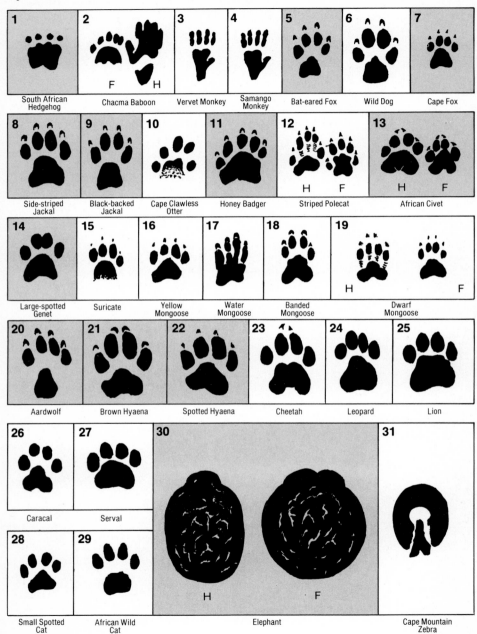

1 South African Hedgehog	**2** Chacma Baboon (F H)	**3** Vervet Monkey	**4** Samango Monkey	**5** Bat-eared Fox	**6** Wild Dog	**7** Cape Fox
8 Side-striped Jackal	**9** Black-backed Jackal	**10** Cape Clawless Otter	**11** Honey Badger	**12** Striped Polecat (H F)	**13** African Civet (H F)	
14 Large-spotted Genet	**15** Suricate	**16** Yellow Mongoose	**17** Water Mongoose	**18** Banded Mongoose	**19** Dwarf Mongoose (H F)	
20 Aardwolf	**21** Brown Hyaena	**22** Spotted Hyaena	**23** Cheetah	**24** Leopard	**25** Lion	

26 Caracal
27 Serval
28 Small Spotted Cat
29 African Wild Cat
30 Elephant (H F)
31 Cape Mountain Zebra

180

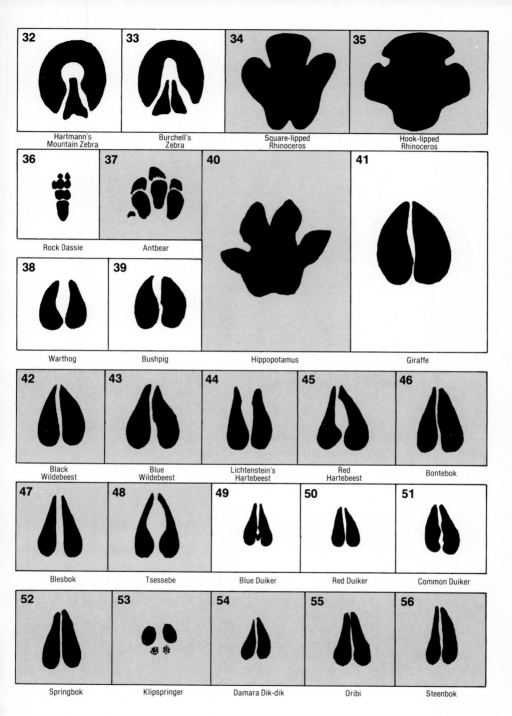

32 Hartmann's Mountain Zebra

33 Burchell's Zebra

34 Square-lipped Rhinoceros

35 Hook-lipped Rhinoceros

36 Rock Dassie

37 Antbear

40 Hippopotamus

41 Giraffe

38 Warthog

39 Bushpig

42 Black Wildebeest

43 Blue Wildebeest

44 Lichtenstein's Hartebeest

45 Red Hartebeest

46 Bontebok

47 Blesbok

48 Tsessebe

49 Blue Duiker

50 Red Duiker

51 Common Duiker

52 Springbok

53 Klipspringer

54 Damara Dik-dik

55 Oribi

56 Steenbok

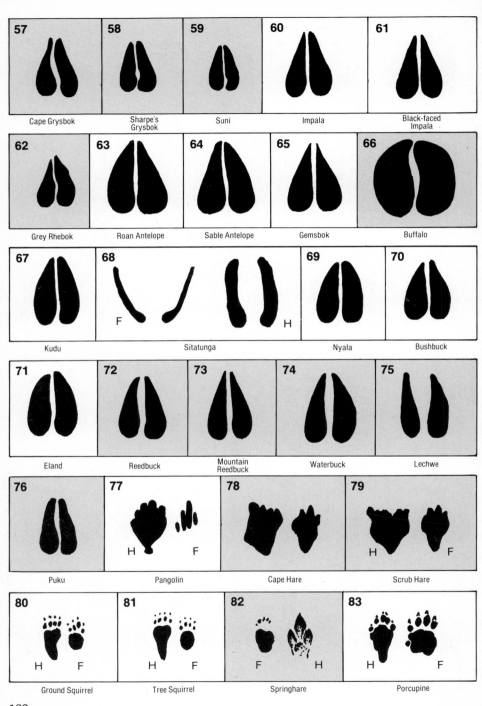

57 Cape Grysbok	**58** Sharpe's Grysbok	**59** Suni	**60** Impala	**61** Black-faced Impala
62 Grey Rhebok	**63** Roan Antelope	**64** Sable Antelope	**65** Gemsbok	**66** Buffalo
67 Kudu	**68** Sitatunga		**69** Nyala	**70** Bushbuck
71 Eland	**72** Reedbuck	**73** Mountain Reedbuck	**74** Waterbuck	**75** Lechwe
76 Puku	**77** Pangolin	**78** Cape Hare	**79** Scrub Hare	
80 Ground Squirrel	**81** Tree Squirrel	**82** Springhare	**83** Porcupine	

182